MAHARAJAH DEVI SINHA AND THE NASHIPUR RAJ

MAHARAJAH DEVI SINHA AND THE NASHIPUR RAJ

DEMETRIUS C. BOULGER

GYAN

Published by

GYAN

Gyan Publishing House
5, Ansari Road
Daryaganj, New Delhi-110002
Phone: 011-47034999, 9811692060
E-mail: books@gyanbooks.com

Distribution Network
gyanbooks.com
India, USA, Canada, UK, Australia

ISBN: 978-93-7447-206-4 (PB)

First Published, 1912

2nd Impression 2026

Printed at: Gyan Press, Delhi.

MAHARAJAH DEVI SINHA AND THE NASHIPUR RAJ
Author: DEMETRIUS C. BOULGER

MAHARAJAH DEVI SINHA AND THE NASHIPUR RAJ

BY

DEMETRIUS C. BOULGER

AUTHOR OF "INDIA IN THE NINETEENTH CENTURY," ETC.

WITH 15 ILLUSTRATIONS

"Despise no one"

MOTTO OF NASHIPUR

PUBLISHED BY THE AUTHOR AT

12, BLOOMSBURY SQUARE, LONDON, W.C.

1912

PREFACE

The present Maharajah Bahadur of Nashipur in Bengal, being desirous that it should be made clear that the charges brought against his predecessor in the eighteenth century, Maharajah Devi Sinha, were disproved at the time they were made, has entrusted me with the task of preparing the following narrative.

Devi Sinha's name figured prominently in the earlier stages of the Warren Hastings trial, but Burke, finding that his "alleged enormities" were rebutted, dropped that part of his "charges."

It is proper to mention that Chapters III. and IV. are based on documents collected by Professor A. F. Murison, LL.D., from the Bengal Minute Books in the India Office Library.

I have added to the story of Devi Sinha a description of the Nashipur Raj down to the present day, and in regard to this part of the work I must thank Babu Surada Prosad Mukerjee, B.A., Dewan of Nashipur Raj, for the information and materials with which he has supplied me.

DEMETRIUS C. BOULGER.

H.H. THE MAHARAJAH BAHADUR OF NASHIPUR.

CONTENTS

LIST OF ILLUSTRATIONS

MAHARAJAH DEVI SINHA AND THE NASHIPUR RAJ

CHAPTER I

THE ANCIENT FAMILY OF NASHIPUR

STUDENTS who have occasion to examine the records of the East India Company during the seventeenth and eighteenth centuries will find frequent reference therein to "the country powers." By this term is meant not only the great ruling Princes, but the minor notabilities, long indigenous to the soil, who administered the land on behalf of the Mogul Emperors. One of the secrets of the Company's success, in establishing itself in India, was the skill with which it propitiated this class and converted them gradually into firm and loyal allies. The Company was more scrupulous in the observance of its engagements than the Emperor, its policy was based on the maintenance of local right and interest, and thus confidence in its good word was established. It also rewarded good and loyal service generously, and thus made it worth the while of those who worked for it to prove staunch in their fealty. It was in the Presidency of Bengal, more than in any other division of India, that these cordial relations were established with the class comprehensively described in the term, "the country powers."

Among such powers, the family of Nashipur, which is the subject of this narrative, might be accorded a leading place. In antiquity, it is entitled to rank among the noblest families of the peninsula; by loyal service it has been attached to the English for nearly two centuries, and its present representative is a man who has gained distinction in the administrative and legislative fields of public activity. In recognition of his worth, he has been accorded the highest Hindu title of Maharajah, and his influence for good extends far beyond the limits of his own possessions.

The Maharajah comes of very ancient and high lineage. His ancestor, the Maharajah Tarawah, was the ruling chief of Bejapur ("the City of Victory"), in the Deccan, in the fourteenth century A.D. As is explained in the Persian narrative, of which a translation appears a little further on in this chapter, Tarawah, moved by religious considerations, was seized with a desire to see other parts of the Peninsula. He set out with his son, Prince Madan Sinha, and a large following, in Sambat 1352, for the purpose of making a pilgrimage to Kurukshetra, a famous shrine near Umballah in the Punjab. He apparently had no such intention when he started, but, none the less, he had left the Deccan for ever. His brother Maharaoji was left in charge of Bejapur, and probably his descendants were among those who succumbed to the Mahomedans two centuries later, when the Moguls first invaded the Deccan.

Tarawah, having made his pilgrimage, was thinking of returning home, and had marched some distance on his way when the beautiful scenery in which he pitched one of his camps so strongly appealed to him that he decided to found there a new city, to which he gave the name of Taral. This place was situated at no great distance from the Imperial city of Delhi.

While Tarawah was building his new city and consolidating his power, his son, Prince Madan Sinha, who had left Bejapur with him, determined to attend one of the annual festivals in the Temple of Somnath, in Jhind. This ranked among the chief Hindu gatherings in Northern India, and, besides the religious celebrations, it was generally made the occasion of jousts and festivities. In these, Madan Sinha equally distinguished himself by his courage and gaiety. His prowess became the topic of general conversation, and the chief local banker, named Lala Sriram, conceived the idea of arranging a marriage between the young Prince and his daughter, who was famed for her beauty. The banker might have failed in his plans if the young man had not been smitten by what he had been told of the fair one's charms, and, despite his father's objections to the marriage, he declared that he was determined to marry the object of his affections. The Maharajah, seeing his son resolved, withdrew his opposition like a wise man, and the marriage was celebrated with great pomp.

While his son fixed his home in Jhind, the Maharajah continued to rule at Taral, and his reputation as a good ruler became so great that, when the zemindars and jagirdars of a state called Dhanni thought they had reason to complain of their own Rajah's tyranny, they called on Tarawah to redress their grievances. The Maharajah sent his forces to join the discontented party, and several battles were fought with the unpopular Rajah, who was killed in the last of them. The Maharajah appears thereupon to have added Dhanni to his own territory in the way usual among conquerors. Soon after this incident, Tarawah died, and Madan Sinha succeeded to his patrimonial estate at Bejapur, but he had no desire to proceed there, and made an arrangement with his uncle to continue his régime, and to allow him a share of the revenue. This arrangement did not last long, but Madan Sinha possessed his father's territory at Taral, and he also succeeded to the wealth of his father-in-law.

Madan left a son named Sadhu Ram, and he in turn one named Lahar Mal, who had five sons. They were named in their order of birth—Malaraj, Kulchandra, Karanchandra, Devi Sinha, and Lalu Sinha. These five brothers became in course of time very powerful, and extended their influence far and wide. They did not settle in the same place, but separated in search of fresh fields for their activity. Four of them settled respectively in Delhi, Meerut, Mathura, and Thaneswar.

Of the brothers, Kulchandra was the one to settle in Thaneswar, and his second son, Rai Gujarmal, became generalissimo to the Mararajah Scindiah of Gwalior. On one occasion, the Maharajah Scindiah, who had been betrayed by another of his Generals named Ghulam Kader Khan, requested assistance from Rai Shambar Nath and Rai Badir Nath, grandsons of Rai Gujarmal, and it was mainly by their aid and advice that Ghulam Kader Khan was overcome. This added immensely to the family's reputation, and the Mogul Emperor Shah Alum appointed Rai Shambar Nath nazim of the entire tract of country from Shaharanpore to Meerut. He was also made the permanent subadar and fuzdar of Shaharanpore and its dependencies. State officials and the people generally were directed to offer him, as the Emperor's representative, their fealty and allegiance, and also to pay him the Government revenue.

Rai Shambar Nath was able to render some direct aid to the English. In 1803 the East India Company sent a force, under Colonel Burn, to put down some lawless persons in the district, and he invited Rai Shambar to help him, which he promised to do. Among the worst offenders was Rajah Sher Singh, of Buria, in the district of Muzaffir-Nagar. After some fighting, Colonel Burn, not being strong enough, took shelter in a fort with Rai Shambar. It became necessary to summon aid, and this was done, through the Rai's instrumentality, in the manner described in the Persian narrative quoted a little further on.

Rai Sinharaj's descendants, Rai Tarachand and Rai Ajit Sinha, received high posts and honours from the two Emperors Jehangir and Shah Alum respectively, in recognition of their distinguished services.

Another descendant of Rai Sinharaj, named Rai Dewali

Sinha, migrated from Panipat, in the United Provinces, to Bengal, where he settled in the beginning of the eighteenth century, at Sanko Full Bari, near the present station, named Bokhara, on the Azimganj branch line of the East India Railway system. It was his son Devi Sinha who became the founder of the present Nashipur family, as described in the following extract from Major Walsh's "History of Murshidabad." The career and fortunes of Devi Sinha will form the theme of subsequent chapters, but here it will suffice to quote the reference to him from Major Walsh's pages:

"The Nashipur Raj is of some considerable historical interest, and may be traced as far back as Tarachand Sinha of Panipat. Ajit Sinha, grandson of Tarachand, rendered distinguished services under the Mogul Emperor Jehangir.

"Rai Ajit Sinha's eldest son was Amar Sinha, who left four sons, of whom the youngest was Diwali Sinha. Maharajah Devi Sinha Bahadur (who got the title from the Government), the founder of the Nashipur Raj family, was the second son of Diwali; the eldest was Takiram Sinha, and the youngest Bahadur Sinha. In the year A.D. 1756 Devi Sinha migrated from Panipat, the historical battlefield of India to Murshidabad, the capital of Bengal, and for some time carried on business there as a merchant banker. This pursuit he abandoned, however, and took service under the East India Company in the revenue department. He soon held high and responsible offices of trust in connection with the land settlement of Bengal. He was in due course appointed to farm the revenues for the Government of Purmea, and subsequently of Rungpur, Dinajpur, and Edracpur inclusively. In the arrangements made by Warren Hastings in the year 1773, by which Provincial Councils were formed, Devi Sinha became the steward or secretary to the Provincial Council of Murshidabad, and to his charge were committed extensive and populous possessions, yielding an annual revenue of 120 lakhs of rupees."

It will be proper at this stage to give the translation of the Persian history of the family, which contains many interesting details not to be found elsewhere. It reads as follows :

"In many a family it is generally only a few descents that are remembered, and the original head becomes untraceable partly owing to the lapse of some centuries, and partly owing to there being nothing very particular known about him. This family (Nashipur's) stands on a different footing.

"In the first place, a history, still in existence, was written at the beginning, and it has been kept up, although a gap occurs occasionally. Besides, an old member of the family, Rai Kanchaiya Lal who died only in 1910 at the age of seventy-two, not only remembered what he had seen himself, but recollected many old traditions which have proved of great service in this compilation.

"This history would have been more complete and thorough but for the fact that many old sanads were destroyed during the Mutiny of 1857, owing to the mutineers having blown up a house in which they were deposited.

"Maharajah Tarawah, who belonged to the Surajbonsi Rajputs of his day, was the ruling chief of Bejapur, in the Deccan, about Sambat 1352. Among his councillors was a Brahmin by caste, who repeatedly described the spiritual benefits that would arise from a pilgrimage to Kurukshetra, in the Umballa district. It was not an easy task in those days to undertake such a long journey, but, being a religious man, the continued preaching of the Brahmin produced its effect upon him, and the Maharajah resolved to undertake the journey at all costs.

"He accordingly set out on the pilgrimage in Sambat 1352, with great pomp, taking with him his son Kumar

Madan Sinha and a large part of his army, with their followers, and leaving his own brother Maharaoji on the guddee to act in his absence.

"On the return journey he halted at Paniput. The beautfiul scenery of the country simply enchanted him, and he resolved to see more of it. While at Paniput, one Pandi Kesho, a local wealthy Brahmin of great influence, succeeded in approaching and eventually in obtaining the favour of the Maharajah. The Pandi ingratiated himself so much in the Maharajah's favour that the latter promised to make him, and did make him, his family priest. This priest's family still resides at Paniput, and continues to hold the position of priest to the Nashipur family, although it must be remembered that the Nashipur family is spread over many places far distant from one another.

"The Maharajah's desire to see the country being still unabated, he travelled on and arrived at Muzaffurpur, taking his new priest with him. Meantime, the news of a very big religious gathering at a certain temple of Mahadeo in Jhind reached the ears of the young Prince Kumar Madan Sinha. With the kind permission of his illustrious sire, he set out in that direction, taking, of course, such retinue as became his position.

"On the way he had to pass through a dense jungle. Hearing the roars of a tiger, the Prince resolved to kill it himself, and, notwithstanding the remonstrances of his followers, he set out alone in pursuit of the brute, arming himself only with a sword. He succeeded in cutting the tiger in two with a single stroke.

"Thus, the Prince arrived at Jhind in high spirits. Young as he was, he intended to pass his days in merriment, and expressed a desire for a dancing-party, according to the custom generally prevalent in those days, especially in the higher circles. An excellent party was speedily arranged, and he enjoyed it well.

"One Lala Sri Ram, an Ajarwal Kayasht by caste, and a

wealthy local banker, hearing of the youth and valour of the Prince, and tempted by his wealth and pomp, managed to obtain an interview with him with the object of proposing a matrimonial alliance between him and his daughter. He broached the delicate subject in a suitable but cautious manner. Several considerations weighed upon the Prince's mind, but, not liking to give him a rude answer, he referred him to his father.

"The banker wrote to the Maharajah, who did not like the idea, and admonished his son to go to Bejapur; but the Prince, having heard of the matchless beauty of the girl, insisted upon staying there for a little while longer. The Maharajah, on learning of the Prince's intentions, gave his consent to the marriage, as such unions were customary in those days. The ceremony was held with great pomp.

"It is noteworthy that the Rajah of Dhanni—which place was, and is to this day, famous for its breed of horses—began at this time to oppress his subjects. To such an extent did he carry this oppression, that the zemindars and jagirdars became discontented, and Pandi Kesho, the Maharajah's priest, took up their cause and quarrelled with the Rajah. The Maharajah Tarawah, not liking to see his own priest humiliated, took his side and sent a military force of some five thousand men to punish the tyrant. The rival forces came into collision, and a severe conflict ensued, causing some losses on both sides. The Maharajah in the end gained the victory, the Rajah being killed, and his State passed into Tarawah's possession.

"Some time after this incident Maharajah Tarawah died, and his son was proclaimed Rajah of Dhanni. Kumar Madan Sinha did not like to go there himself on account of his marriage with the banker's daughter, and therefore his uncle Rawat ruled there on his behalf, sending him about half the revenue each year.

"God favoured Rao Madan Sinha with a son, who was

named Rao Sadho, but as he was born of a Vaish mother he got the nickname of Mahojon. Further marriages into Vaish families turned this branch into a regular Vaish family.

"The origin and descent from the Maharajah is clearly discernible from the Sakha Chor (names of pedigree) which is veiled by the family puzi on the occasion of every marriage in the family, and in which the names of Maharajah Tarawah and the word "Kharakdhari" (meaning those who handled swords) are prominently mentioned.

"Rao Sadho got a son named Kunwar Nanipal, who in turn had a son named Rai Lahor Mal. The last named had five sons.

"An idea struck the sensitive mind of the Prince Lahor Mal that it was not well to live in the land which his own ancestor had given to the Brahmins. As he had many sons, they settled in different places, among others Delhi, Meerut, and Mahsudabad, now known as Murshidabad.

"Rao Lahor Mal having five sons, and they having settled in different places, nothing is accurately known of some of these branches of the family, nor is it easy to gather information about them after such a long time.

"The narrative, therefore, will be confined to the two branches, the one living at Delhi and the other at Nashipur.

"Among these was Rai Eiyor Mal, who was chief commander of the armies of the Gwalior State. His son Rai Bhani Rai held the post of Mir Munshi under the Emperor of Delhi, and was also put in charge of the Silah Khana and Toshikhana in the Imperial Court. His son was also chief commander to Madho Rao Scindia.

"To turn to the Nashipur branch, lawlessness being the order of the day, the East India Company sent a body of troops to put an end to it. In this task, Lieutenant-Colonel W. Burn had to encounter many foes. He made Rai Shambar Nath his friend, and the Rai accompanied the Colonel on his expedition. This was in A.D. 1803. On the way they encountered Rajah Shri Sing of Buria. Fighting ensued between them at Shambi, with the result that the Colonel and the Rai sahib were besieged in a fort. They remained besieged for three days, and could not hit upon any means of making their escape. Rai Shambar Nath happened to have with him an old confidant, a fakir named Bawa Magui Ram. The Rai obtained from the Colonel a letter for the Begum of Shineru at Sardhana, and he also wrote himself to his own brother Rai Badri Nath, stationed at Meerut. He selected the fakir for the delicate and dangerous mission of speedily delivering these letters. The fakir got out of the fort at night, and made his way in safety first to the Begum, and then to Rai Badri Nath.

"Both promised help, and speedily arranged to send reinforcements. The fakir returned by the same passage through which he had gone out and again at night, and delivered to Rai Shambar Nath the cheerful news of the speedy arrival of the reinforcements. The whole of the next day was spent in anxious suspense, but no friendly troops could be seen. On the third day, however, the suspense was changed to cheerfulness when the reinforcements came into sight. The besieged, thus encouraged, came out of their fort and attacked the besiegers. From the other direction the joined forces of Rai Badri Nath and the Begum of Sardhana carried on the attack, and much carnage ensued. The fighting lasted altogether for three days, Shri Sing being finally routed.

"The victory was not confined to a small tract of country, but it had a very far-reaching effect, since it led to the easy conquest of the whole Dooab (*vide* Report of Mr. T. C. Plowden, Collector at Meerut, November 7, 1842).

"The British General fixed the pay of Rai Badri Nath's bodyguard who had joined Colonel Burn at 20,000 rupees per month, being at the rate of thirty rupees per horseman. He also appointed Rai Shambar Nath to be a Tehsildar of

BABU SURADA PROSAD MUKHOPADHYAY.

Dewan of Nashipur Raj.

To face page 10.

eleven Pargannahs in the Saharanpur district (the Purwana of July 28, 1805)."

Taking the line of Rai Shambar Nath, his son Rai Kelka Nath was also appointed Tehsildar. On the latter's death, his son Rai Bishambar Sahai, being under age, Mr. T. C. Plowden, the Collector, had his nephew Rai Salug Ram appointed Tehsildar. In his report, on this occasion, he brought prominently before the Commissioners the services of Rai Shambar Nath. Rai Bishambar Sahai, the son referred to, subsequently displayed conspicuous loyalty during the Mutiny of 1857 (*vide* Mr. J. C. Wilson's [Commissioner] certificate of March 24, 1858). He in his turn was appointed a Tehsildar. His son Rai Ram Chandar Sahai is now a Deputy-Collector in the United Provinces.

TRANSLATION OF SANADS AND COPIES OF REPORTS, ETC.

Pay of the horsemen of Rai Badri Nath's bodyguard, who joined Colonel Burn in the Battle of Shambi, fixed, by order of the General (commanding the East India Company's forces), from August 1, 1804, at 20,000 rupees a month, at the rate of 30 rupees per horseman per *mensem*.

(Signed) G. D. GUTHRIE.
W. BURN, *Lieutenant-Colonel.*

Purwana from the Collector of Saharanpur appoints Rai Shambar Nath to the office of Tehsildar of eleven Pargannahs (Saharanpur, Mahpies, Feizabad, Sultanpur, Nakor, Jal Karah, Yangah, Sakhmauti, Chauzat Kari, Kontha, and Rampur) from the beginning of 1213 F., and makes him responsible for the levies and safety of the people under his jurisdiction, and charges him with the suppression of the forces and movements of the predatory and marauding tribes.

(Signed) G. D. GUTHRIE,
Collector.

SAHARANPUR,
July 28, 1805.

No. 405.

To A. W. Begbie, Esq., Officiating Commissioner, Meerut Division.

SIR,

I have the honour to report to you the death, on the 19th ult., of Rai Kalka Das, Tehsildar. I have nominated Salug Ram, his nephew, temporarily to the situation, in order to test his qualifications for it. The long and good services of his deceased uncle and his grandfather, Rai Shambar Nath, who was Vazir of the whole tract from Saharanpur to Meerut under the native government at the time the Dooab was conquered by us, added to his own good character, give him a claim which I hope you will agree with me in thinking ought to be recognised if on trial he be found fit for the situation.

I have, etc.,

T. C. PLOWDEN,

November 7, 1842. *Collector.*

I hereby certify that Bishambar Sahai, Vazir of the Meerut Collectorate, was ordered by Mr. Dunlop, the Magistrate and Collector, to attend upon me during the rebellion. He obeyed the order, and I employed him until the close of the year 1857. I found him attentive and hard-working. He accompanied me to the Hauffer expedition, and, when it was resolved that the Hauffer force should proceed to the Muzaffir Noyo district, Bishambar Sahai accompanied me there also. I should be glad if promotion and emolument could be found for him, for he certainly behaved well when every native official was more or less paralyzed by fear.

J. C. WILSON,

Commissioner on Special Duty.

MEERUT,

March 24, 1858.

CHAPTER II

RAJAH DEVI SINHA

Eighth in descent from Maharajah Tarawah came Rai Tara-chand, otherwise known as Rai Joymal. He and his son, Rai Agajit Sinha, were highly honoured and trusted by the Mogul Emperors, Jehangir and Shah Jehan, to whom they rendered distinguished services. Agajit Sinha's grandson, Rai Dewali Sinha, emigrated soon after the celebrated Battle of Panipat, and established his seat in Bengal at a place not very remote from the present Nashipur, thus beginning the history of the Raj rather over one hundred and sixty years ago. Rai Dewali Sinha is chiefly memorable, however, as the father of Rajah Devi Sinha.

Devi Sinha entered the service of the East India Company either immediately before or just after the Battle of Plassey. He is stated to have rendered Clive some useful service on that occasion, and probably this was in connection with the financial arrangements that followed with Mir Jaffier. As Devi Sinha was intimately acquainted with the revenue arrangements of the Mogul Government, he became a most useful coadjutor of the English, who for the first time were confronted with the task of getting in a revenue from the land. For twenty years or more he served us in this capacity, and then, under the new system, he took upon himself the responsibility of farming the revenue for a specified number of districts in Bengal. This was the transition period when the English passed from simple merchants to the position of the responsible administrators of the country.

At that time, the East India Company had not the staff to collect taxes direct from the people, or even to control the collection by native officials. It therefore adopted the system of sub-letting the collection of the revenue to a farmer, who agreed to pay a lump sum for a specified number of years, generally limited to two, but renewable on good results. In this capacity, Rajah Devi Sinha did excellent service, and no farmer of the revenue stood in higher repute with the authorities than he did. His contracts were for larger sums than any others, and he always kept faith with the Government. The authorities at Calcutta knew, therefore, that from Devi Sinha they would receive the best and the surest results. This reputation led not only to their constantly employing him, but, as the sequel will show, to their thrusting employments upon him which he did not seek, and he thus incurred one of the penalties that attend the too successful man. A difficult charge was thrust upon him, and, despite his reluctance to do so, he had to accept.

Having been for twenty-five years in the State employment, and closely connected all the time with the getting in of the revenue, Rajah Devi Sinha became a man of the highest consideration in Bengal. He also amassed considerable wealth, and added greatly to his paternal estate. His only brother, Rajah Bahadur Sinha Bahadur, was also a great territorial magnate, but he did not concern himself in revenue matters, like his elder brother—in the sense, at least, of incurring responsibility. He had his own extensive estates, he served as a revenue officer, but nothing would induce him to accept the responsibility of a farmer of the revenue, and in this he showed his wisdom. There was no family of higher consideration in the Pargannahs extending from Rungpur to Dinajpur, and including a great part of the modern Kuch Behar. As a consequence

Rajah Devi Sinha was not merely welcomed as a farmer by the Government, but he was always accepted as his own security, and from first to last he never made default in his undertakings, and sometimes, as he said himself, he had to make good the deficiency out of his own pocket.

In those days, the East India Company never attempted to bestow honours on Indians. The most it ever did was to present a khillat (dress of honour) and to recognize existent titles. But it could confer posts, and in 1781 it made Devi Sinha the Dewan, or Governor, of certain districts set forth in the following purwannah:

> "Whereas the office of Dewan of Havely, Peenjerah, etc., and Pargannah Edrachpore, etc., has been conferred on Rajah Devi Sinha by the Huzzoor, it is required that, having performed the duties of his station with integrity and uprightness, he fail not in the smallest degree in diligence and attention. Let his behaviour be such as to render the body of the people happy and contented, and let him take care that the Farmer collects the revenues and transmits them to the Presidency.
>
> "Let him in conducting the business of his Department afford the customary support to the Farmer and promote the improvement of the country, because such a conduct will redound to his honour and be productive of much credit to him."

Shortly after this appointment, the Government, wishing to derive a large revenue from the Rungpur and adjacent districts, bethought themselves of Rajah Devi Sinha as a man likely to increase it. They offered him the post of farmer, and in such a form as showed that he was not expected to refuse. He therefore accepted the charge, but with much reluctance, as he tells us in one of his depositions: he did it out of loyalty to his employers. The two years of his contract were the equivalent of our years 1781 and 1782 (or thereabouts, for they slightly overlapped), and he undertook to provide an increased revenue as the Huzzoor, or Government, desired. He farmed the revenue at a fixed total, which he had to, and, as a matter of fact, did provide. Naturally, great liberty had to be left to the farmer, and the Government never interfered with his methods so long as there was no disturbance. No doubt there were some harsh farmers, but, by the testimony of the majority of witnesses, Devi Sinha was not one of them, and towards the ryots he was admitted to be just and considerate. Indeed, his relations were not with the ryots themselves, but with the zemindars, or landlords. It was from the latter that he levied the taxes, and it is not unimportant to remember that he had no direct relations with the ryots, who may be described as the peasants or the tillers of the soil.

So far as the year 1781 was concerned, the arrangement worked smoothly. The taxes came in regularly, and the farmer was able to hand over his full total to the Government Treasury without loss to himself. But the second year proved disastrous to the farmer and unsatisfactory to the Government. The zemindars wished to evade some of their obligations, and the ryots were cajoled into concurring in a diminution of rent, and at the same time incurring an obligation to make up the difference to the landowner in the form of special taxes called *derinwillah* and *battah*. In 1782, a complete change took place also in market prices, and consequently in the material condition of the people. Owing not to scarcity, but to the abundance of the harvests, prices fell, and the ryots were unable to sell their grain and tobacco. Then they resented the payment of the extra taxes levied surreptitiously by the zemindars, and refused to pay them. Their discontent could not be appeased, and soon assumed the form of open insurrection in Rungpur and Dinajpur.

This incident attracted the attention of Government, and a civilian was sent to Rungpur to inquire into the affair. It was not difficult to learn that the ryots were discontented, and they alleged that they had genuine grievances in the levying of the new taxes named. The civilian, Mr. Paterson, pricked up his ears at the mention of new taxes, and at once jumped to the conclusion that the farmer Rajah Devi Sinha must be the culprit. He also received a miscellaneous assortment of evidence as to acts of cruelty, and there was never any doubt or uncertainty that cruelty was freely resorted to by the tax-collector in the Mogul realm. Cruelty in the collection of State dues was not restricted to India or Asia; in the eighteenth century it was common throughout Europe. But if Mr. Paterson had inquired a little more closely, he could not have failed to find that Rajah Devi Sinha had the reputation of being an indulgent "farmer," and that whenever he came into direct contact with the ryots—which was seldom—he treated them with kindness and consideration. Indeed, if the situation had been carefully considered, it would have been clear to him that the interests of the farmer were closely connected with those of the ryots, and that a state of insurrection menaced the farmer with ruin.

The following accounts of the insurrection in 1782 show that it was serious enough while it lasted:

"In the various depositions taken before the Commission in their inquiry into the causes of the insurrection from the busneahs, putwarries, etc., they universally attribute the insurrection to the want of money to pay their revenue, which want of money is as universally attributed to the total stagnation of all trade: there being little sale of the various articles produced in the district in 1188, and much less in the year 1189 (Bengal years equivalent to A.D. 1781-82). This want of money occasioned by the want of purchasers rendered the ryots incapable of discharging their revenues, and though we could not learn that any excessive severities, similar to those inflicted by Hurram in 1188, were used to enforce the payment of the revenue in 1189, yet when the great arrears due to the Rajah from the several zemindars and under-farmers, and the near expiration of his lease, were considered, it must be concluded that the usual severities of punishment and confinement were used to make the zemindars pay up their revenues, and that the zemindars punished and confined the under-farmers and ryots to make them both pay up their revenue. . . .

"The ryots first met at ——. In consequence of a plan concerted there among themselves they assembled, and from thence they proceeded to Kymarry, in Tapah, where by the evidence of ——, Deijenarrain offered to head them, and he was chosen their nabob with shouts of approbation. Deijenarrain is the son of Doolub Narrain, who had acted as nabob in an insurrection which formerly took place in this district about twenty-five years ago, on which account he was elected the nabob of the late insurrection.

"After this, the insurgents sent twenty-five or thirty men to Dakally Gunge, who released such people as were confined there for revenue. The ryots of the neighbouring talooks assembled, and came to them in great numbers, and presented their nuzzars to Deijenarrain. Deijenarrain mounted a palanquin, and they proceeded to Balagong, where, by the advice of ——, it was proposed to go to Demlah, where Gourmohun was, whom they considered as having treated them with great severity.

"The insurgents then circulated letters to the various talooks, ordering the ryots to assemble and join them, and threatening to burn their houses and burn their crops in case of their refusal and delay. The insurgents determined to go to Demlah, where they were told that there were horsemen and burcandasses stationed at Demlah who would attack them, and therefore it was of little purpose to go there; but, however, he proposed that the insurgents should go there, and if they obtained redress it was very well, but if Gourmohun should attack them they would repel his attack, telling Deijenarrain that, as he was nabob, he must forgive them for what excesses ("loutmar"), plunder, and murder were committed. That Deijenarrain considered for some time, and replied that they did not go to fight, but were going for justice; that if Gourmohun refused them justice and attacked them, that they must do the best they could, and that he forgave all excesses ("lootmar"), plunder, and murder.

"On this the people all shouted and proceeded towards Demlah, where they found horsemen and burcandasses drawn up. The insurgents stopped, and Deijenarrain quitted his palanquin. The insurgents beat their drums and advanced. When they had approached within half a mile of the burcandasses, the insurgents gave the Duvy, declaring they came for justice, but not to fight. The burcandasses gave them encouragement, and promised them justice. They therefore advanced about the distance of an arrow's flight, when a gun was fired by the burcandasses, and one man was killed on the part of the insurgents, on which they began to fly; but, observing that other parties had arrived from the southward and westward, they returned and killed two of the burcandasses. The horsemen and burcandasses fled, and report was made that Gourmohun was taken. Deijenarrain said: 'Take care of him; he is a Brahmin. *Marrow mut* (Do not kill or beat him).'

"On this the insurgents attacked Deijenarrain, who retired to a distance, and Gourmohun was killed by the insurgents.

"More burcandasses being reported, the insurgents retired to the banks of a river; but on the sight of some horsemen approaching, they fled. Some were taken by the horsemen, and some houses were burnt.

"After this, Keenah Sirdar was appointed nabob of the insurgents. As they were going to Sarabary they saw Goculmattah stationed on the banks of a tank near the haut when they gave the duvy, and said: 'Give us justice! Why do you come to kill us?' Goculmattah beckoned to them to come, and told them he would give them redress. Whereupon some of them threw down their clubs, and others put them under their arms, and were going to him. When they had approached within an arrow's flight, the burcandasses and horsemen discharged their arrows and guns at them, and wounded two ryots, on which the insurgents surrounded and attacked Goculmattah, killing him and two burcandasses.

"The ryots in Dinagepore assembled, beat their amlah, plundered the cutcherry of what revenue was collected and deposited there, and carried off with them the papers and the amlah to Chenglee, where they were attacked and dispersed by Mirza Mahomed Tuckey, who was sent to suppress them by order of Mr. Goodlad. The ringleaders were sent to Rungpore, and the remainder were sent or returned to their homes.

"Notwithstanding the declaration of the ryots that they would rather return to their homes, they only separated for a time and assembled in different parts, murdered Goculmattah, who had arrived only three days in the district to carry on the collections. As they continued assembling, Mr. Goodlad then ordered the officer whom he had sent with sepoys to attack the insurgents and disperse them. *The officer attacked them and killed many of them,* and they dispersed when the district was, in consequence of this action, reduced to quiet and obedience."

The description of the circumstances of the rising, given by Mr. Goodlad, Collector of Rungpur, supplements that provided by the Commission of Inquiry, and may be quoted here:

"In the month of April, 1781, I was appointed Collector of Rungpore, and in the same month a general settlement of the lands took place. The provinces of Rungpore, Dinagepore, and Goragaut were given in farm at an increased rent to Rajah Devi Sinha for the term of two years, and the farmer was placed under my superintendence. During the first year the farmer fulfilled his engagements to Government with a punctuality superior to any other

THE NOTMANDIR.

Opposite the big temple at Nashipur.

To face page 29.

renter in Bengal. In the second year (though the settlement of Rungpore made by the farmer with his underwriters was near half a lakh of rupees less than his engagements with Government), towards the expiration of his lease, part of the district rose in arms against him when not half the revenue of the year was realized, murdered such of his officers as they could seize, erected a nabob and government among themselves, raised contributions, marched through sundry parts of the district in arms, compelled such natives as were peaceably inclined to join them in opposition to all authority, and by proclamation forbid all payments of revenue to Government.

"To quell so formidable an insurrection, I was obliged, after trying every lenient measure, to have recourse to military aid. Some lives were lost, but in about a month I had the happiness to subdue the insurgents, and restore peace to the district."

These narratives may be completed by the following extracts from the reply made by the Rajah Devi Sinha when the charges were brought against him in July, 1783. It is perfectly clear, from the tone and language of the letter, that he had no consciousness of guilt, and that he did not at that moment realize the severe ordeal that lay before him:

"I have received the committee's purwannah, directing me to deliver in my answer to several articles of complaint which Mr. Paterson has transmitted to them, and am very glad that they have afforded me this opportunity of vindicating myself against the false representations of my enemies.

"From the first day of my appointment to Rungpore to the time when I was suspended from my employment in the transaction of my business, I have never deviated from the principles of equity and moderation, but have strictly adhered to the orders of the Huzzoor and the custom of the country, all which on inquiry I am conscious will appear. Be pleased to consider, gentlemen, by whom the complaints against me have been preferred. The complainants are for the most part the zemindars, who themselves, long before my arrival in that part of the country, were guilty of many of the oppressions of which they at present accuse me, every species of mathoat having been imposed by them, and the cultivation of the country thereby greatly impeded. Besides, the zemindars imagined that, by complaining in this manner, they would avoid the payment of their balances, and in fact they have accomplished their object, for from the time of Mr. Paterson's arrival at Rungpore the sum of 1,000 rupees has not been collected.

"When the year 1189 was nearly expired, and the zemindars also knew that my lease was only for the two years, and saw that I exerted myself in my business at the very time of the heavy collections, they created disturbances and put a total stop to them, and notwithstanding that Mr. Goodlad issued orders directing all those who thought themselves aggrieved to make their complaints known to him so that they should be redressed, they paid no regard thereto, but spread confusion and disorder throughout the whole district.

"When the report was first circulated that Mr. Paterson was coming to inquire into the disturbances, I considered his deputation as a favourable event to me, and depended upon his support in realizing the balances; but in this I was disappointed, for he has received the false complaints of the zemindars, transmitted them to the Committee, and not afforded me the least assistance in recovering the balances. By the complaints which have been sent down, my reputation has been greatly affected. Be assured, gentlemen, that on inquiry they will never be found capable of proof.

"You are also acquainted with the custom of the country, and know that when a European ameen is deputed on any business into the Mofussil, the whole country comes to him to complain, because the zemindars and ryots look upon this as a favourable opportunity, and make complaints to him, right or wrong, with the view that the payment of their balances will not be enforced. This happened when Mr. Paterson came to Rungpore.

"The zemindars instigated the ryots into an insurrection, and the insurgents set fire to the sagawal's cutchery, joined the nabobs of the Dhing, murdered Gourmohun, Goculmattah, etc., seized and carried off the Company's revenues, and took refuge at Serrooppore, a place forming the boundary of two districts."

The same purwannah from the Rajah contains a full examination of the financial points of the case and his replies thereto, but as they will be dealt with in the next chapter it is unnecessary to quote them textually here.

The explanation of the trouble which befell the Rajah, and which will be set forth in the following chapters by a summary of the Government's proceedings, is to be found, first, in Mr. Paterson's ignorance of local customs, and, secondly, in his desire to obtain personal notoriety by probing to its root what seemed to be a scandal. His information was derived from the zemindars and the ryots amenable to their authority, and it was quite easy to make out a plausible case against the farmer of the taxes. There had undoubtedly been a popular rising attended with some bloodshed and considerable loss to the Company's revenue, and, as tranquillity was the first essential from the Government's point of view, a scapegoat was sought and found in Rajah Devi Sinha. Indeed, if Mr. Paterson had confined his attacks to the Rajah, there is no saying that he would not have succeeded in imposing his will on the supreme Council, but fortunately for Devi Sinha he attacked everybody—the Collector, Mr. Goodlad, the Commissioners, and even the governing Board.

For a time, however, it seemed as if he would carry

everything in his own way. Rajah Devi Sinha was removed from his post and ordered to Calcutta, where he was kept in waiting over a year before he knew what he was charged with. Mr. Goodlad, the Rungpur Collector, was also suspended and summoned to Calcutta to explain his proceedings. Mr. Paterson appealed to the public conscience against the enormities he had discovered, and many persons were more or less frightened. Indeed, the Governor-General's Council treated the worst tirades of Mr. Paterson with marvellous forbearance, seeing that they did not escape from his shafts as well as others. It was very fortunate that communications between India and England then took six months, and that there was no sensational press to descant on the forms of compulsion to which recalcitrant taxpayers were subjected under the Mogul system which in 1781-82 had not been disturbed. A few strong men held out at the beginning against Mr. Paterson's insinuations. Sir John Shore, President of the Board of Revenue, declared that they were no evidence against Devi Sinha. But the Governor-General's Council, after taking fifteen months to consider the matter, decided to institute an inquiry, which will be described in the next chapter. The public opinion of England, the party strife of the House of Commons, had not yet embraced Indian questions, but the shadow of the Hastings indictment already began to obscure the air.

CHAPTER III

THE CHARGES AGAINST DEVI SINHA

In the report of the trial of Warren Hastings at the bar of the House of Lords there are repeated references by the prosecuting counsel to the "enormities" of Devi Sinha, or, as it is spelt in the Minutes of Evidence, "Deby Sing."* The case for the prosecution being that Warren Hastings was a monster, it was necessary to support it by showing that he had hireling monsters under him, and one of those fixed upon was Devi Sinha. The prosecuting counsel having shown an intention to bring in "the enormities of Deby Sing" as being equivalent to "the enormities of Warren Hastings," the Lord Chancellor ruled that "it was not competent for them to give evidence of the enormities actually committed by Deby Sing, the same not being charged in the impeachment." But, the ruling notwithstanding, the Court was regaled with a pretty full history of his doings and alleged misdeeds, and the following narrative of the true case as rebutting the slander is compressed from the official papers. The result, as in the case of Warren Hastings, must be regarded as a full acquittal.

It may be interesting, before setting forth the case according to the evidence and particulars collected and put forward in Bengal, to give a sample of Burke's denunciation of the unfortunate Hindu gentleman whom, without any possibility of defending himself, he wished to brand for

* In the report of the trial and generally throughout the records of the time the Rajah's name is spelt Deby Sing.

all time with infamy. He accuses him first of indulging "in the humble, sneaking, suppliant tone of an accused person," and then becoming so bold and confident that he constituted himself "Mr. Paterson's accuser." The documents quoted hereafter will give the reader the means of forming his own opinion on the subject; but, even in the Court, Mr. Burke's indictment failed to reach its mark, for Mr. Edward Law (afterwards the first Lord Ellenborough), leading counsel for the defence, denounced "what I will call the very shocking and atrocious fable of Deby Sing."

But it was Hastings himself who gave, in a speech of great moderation, the death-blow to Burke's romance. The following are the pertinent passages from the Governor-General's answers to the charges:

"My Lords, I will not detain your Lordships by adverting for any length to the story told by the Manager (Burke), who opened the general charge relative to the horrid cruelties practised on the natives of Dheejumla by Deby Sing. It will be sufficient to say that the Manager never ventured to introduce this story in the form of a charge, though pressed and urged to do so in the strongest possible terms both in and out of Parliament.

"Mr. Paterson, on whose authority he relied for the truth of his assertions, and with whom he said he wished to go down to posterity, has had the generosity to write to my attorney in Calcutta, for my information, that he felt the sincerest concern to find his reports turned to my disadvantage, as I had acted as might be expected from a man of humanity throughout all the transactions in which Deby Sing was concerned.

"Had the cruelties which the Manager stated really been inflicted, it was not possible, as he very well knew at the time, to impute them even by any kind of forced construction to me.

"My Lords, it is a fact that I was the first person to give Mr. Paterson an ill-opinion of Deby Sing, whose conduct upon former occasions had left an unfavourable and, perhaps, an unjust impression upon my mind. In employing Deby Sing, I certainly yielded up my opinion to that of Mr. Anderson and Mr. Shore, *who had better opportunities of knowing him than I could have.*

"In the course of the inquiry into his conduct, he received neither favour nor countenance from me nor from any member of the Board. That inquiry was carried on principally when I was at Lucknow, and was not completed during my government, though it was commenced and continued with every possible solemnity, and with the sincerest desire on my part and on the part of my colleagues to do strict and impartial justice.

"The result I have read in England; and it certainly appears that, though the man was not entirely innocent, the extent of his guilt bore no sort of proportion to the magnitude of the charges against him. In particular, it proved that the most horrible of those horrible acts, so artfully detailed and with such effect in this place, *never were committed at all.*

"Here I leave the subject, convinced that every one of your lordships must feel for the unparalleled injustice that was done to me by the introduction and propagation of that atrocious calumny."

We will now proceed to tell the story of Devi Sinha's ordeal from the official Minutes and Proceedings of the Bengal Government. It is told here for the first time.

The perusal of the last chapter must have shown that Devi Sinha was a remarkable man. Otherwise, he could never have held the rarely combined offices of "Farmer of the Revenue, Security, and Dewan." The counsel for the prosecution alleged that such a combination had never been allowed before, but this assertion only betrayed ignorance of Indian facts, for the combination of farmer and security in one person was quite common, and, in at least one other case, the position of dewan had been combined with them.

The evidence on this point given by Mr. John Shore, afterwards Lord Teignmouth, is conclusive. He wrote:

"Rajah Deby Sing was farmer, security, and dewan of Rungpore. The union of the two former offices in the same person requires no explanation, since the practice is very general, and is founded upon solid and obvious reasons. The investiture of the office of dewan during the period in which he held the farm is less common, but not without a precedent, for Rajah Cullyan Singh stood precisely in the same predicament with regard to the Province of Behar."

With regard to the insinuation of Mr. Paterson (who was certainly the originator of the scandal), the Council said: "The imputations thrown out by Mr. Paterson on the grounds of this appointment appear to us of little consequence. The reasons are deduced from conjectures, not from facts."

The first point to be established is, that however rarely the duly qualified person presented himself, there was nothing unwarrantable in Warren Hastings entrusting such a man as Devi Sinha with a double or treble office.

One of the first charges against Devi Sinha was that, in the last year of his holding office, he had collected a sum of about 19,704 rupees from one pargannah, and put it down to the accounts of the previous year. This was alleged to be proof of his squeezing the people and extorting money to which he had no right. The Council at Fort William, without waiting for fuller information, decided that Devi Sinha was in the wrong, and called upon him to pay in the 19,704 rupees to the Treasury. This the Rajah expressed his willingness to do under protest, and his defence reads like that of an honest man:

"I am directed, in consequence of the orders from the gentlemen of the Council at Calcutta, to pay the sum of 19,704.10 rupees, being the revenue of 1182, on account of the Mehals of the Chuckla Akbunagur, collected by me and brought to the account of 1181. I answer that I collected 2994.4.10 Sicca rupees, on account of the revenue 1182, in which year the Mehals were under the care of my officers to the end of Bhadon, and have rendered the accounts to the mutsuddin of Nabob Ehteram-ud-Dowlah, as appears by the chelaun, which I can produce under the signature of Mofussil officers, who took in return a receipt from the officers belonging to me. If there are any errors in these accounts I am ready to render them again. Besides the sum above mentioned, of which I have rendered an account, I did not collect a daum of the revenue of 1182. If the contrary can, on examination, be proved, I am ready to answer it.

"But one thing that the mutsuddies of the Nabob Ehteram-ud-Dowlah dispute about: in the three pargannahs of Botteah, etc., which are included in the pargannah of Rajemehal, it is customary for the collection to commence at the beginning of Sauwun and to be finished at the end of Assar, and agreeably to this I collected, and the nabob will do himself the same in future. His mutsuddies, notwithstanding this, want the collections made from those three Mehals to be inserted contrary to the established usage among the Aumdunny of 1182. When this shall be examined into, you will, by attending to the established custom, perceive the injustice of it, for I made the collections and dispatches in the same manner as was done in Mr. Harwood's time, and this is agreeably to the usage of the country in many places.

"The Mehals in question were, in Mr. Harwood's time, under the management of Roy Dulul Ram, and he likewise went on agreeably to this custom. He is now present; let an inquiry be made of him, or else let the examination be entrusted by the Council to the Khalsa Shereefa, or to the decisions of the Comongoe's offices. Whatsoever shall be decided agreeably to the Sudder and Mofussil papers, and according to the established custom, I will abide by."

Mr. Cleveland, the local collector, was consulted, and bore out Devi Sinha's statement, adding that, "by the custom of the country, he was undoubtedly entitled to do what he had done." Incidentally he let out the secret of the trouble. The pernicious custom of anticipating the revenue was put a stop to a year or so after Devi's retirement, with the consequence that his successor would have been in the end the loser of part of a year's revenue. The Council, having satisfied themselves that there was no case against Devi Sinha, and at the same time that it would be very hard on his successor to lose the money, directed that the balance be written off, and credit given for the amount to the new farmer.

The next charge against Devi Sinha related to the disturbances at Rungpur, a large zemindari which he rented through a nominee, named Comal Uddin Hussein.

This occurrence is described in the following passage from the official report on the subject.

"On February 6, 1783, we received a letter from the Collector of Rungpore, dated January 27, communicating the first information of an alarming disturbance which had arisen in the Province, and had become general; that the insurgents had murdered one of the Mofussil gomastahs, named Gouranmohun; that the insurrection had begun without the least notice, or even the smallest complaint; and by a subsequent letter, dated February 6, we were informed that the ryots had chosen a nabob or chief of the insurrection, and compelled others to join them; that a military force had been employed against them, and that the disturbance was not suppressed without great opposition and the loss of many lives. It appearing to us a very uncommon and extraordinary disturbance, we deemed it our indispensable duty to order a particular investigation of the causes and nature of it.

"For this purpose we invested Mr. Paterson with a special commission, and deputed him to Rungpore. At the same time, the most positive directions were sent to the collector and farmer to co-operate with and assist him in his inquiries.

"As the object of this investigation was to ascertain whether the inhabitants of a whole district were driven to resistance and insurrection by the oppression and severity of the farmer, Rajah Devi Sinha, and his agents; or whether they were instigated to rise in arms from the hope of protracting and ultimately evading the demands upon them for rent; it is to be regretted that Mr. Paterson's inquiries do not furnish proofs sufficiently accurate to enable us to decide with certainty upon a matter so important in its consequences."

The charges brought by the zemindars of Rungpur against Rajah Devi Sinha, whose proceedings were alleged to be the cause of the local disturbances, were divided under seven heads. They were:

1. Increasing the Jumma beyond the ability of country to pay.

2. Compelling the zemindars to sign engagements for the revenue of their respective zemindaris, and afterwards confining them and employing other persons in making the collections.

3. Imposition of various taxes over and above the Jumma.

4. Deducting large sums from the receipts.

5. Charging exorbitant batta, and short weight, by which means the demands for revenue were increased, the weight of which fell ultimately on the ryots.

6. Selling the talooks, cammar lands, etc., at an under value.

7. Excessive severities exercised to compel payment of the demands of revenue.

With regard to the first charge, which may be defined as affecting an increase amounting to 86,489 rupees, the Rajah admitted the facts, but readily offered an explanation, which seemed to show that he at least was not ashamed of them. His explanation reads as follows:

"A Mofussil settlement is never realized. Great expenses are incurred by employing people in the collections, and paying interest for money; that, after paying his revenue and defraying those charges and the loss he is liable to sustain from other quarters, the residue would not be a sum disproportionate to his trouble and risk under such extensive engagements."

This explanation was accepted as reasonable because, as noted, "Devi Sinha did not receive any allowance as farmer." His salary and allowance as dewan were 9,045 rupees a year.

We come now to the second charge of compelling the zemindars to sign, and of then confining them. The situation cannot be made clearer than by epitomizing the official report.

In the first place, the term "zemindars" was not used accurately in the list of charges. It was employed as if they acted themselves, whereas among them were many women and children, and the majority of the others employed dewans as representatives. One of these was named Gourmohun, and in Assar 1188 he signed a settlement at Dinajpur with Devi Sinha for the zemindari of Carjeehaut. This settlement was not deemed satisfactory by the zemindar, who went himself to Dinajpur to have it altered. Instead of this object being attained, he agreed to sign it himself, and Gourmohun was dismissed from his post as general dewan of the zemindari body. This mark of displeasure did not prove all that it seemed to imply, for a few weeks later Gourmohun was reinstated in his old office, but it gave colour to the story that the zemindar of Carjeehaut and others had been coerced into ratifying a settlement to which they were really averse. The official verdict on this point was the only one possible: "As no proofs have been laid before us of the force complained of by the zemindars to extort those writings from them or their agents, we must consider them as valid until the alleged force shall be fully proved."

Devi Sinha's version of the facts was that the zemindars came to him voluntarily, that he never interfered in the collection which was managed by the zemindars and their agents, and finally that a man named Hurram, "by the zemindars' appointment and by his own bond," had become security, and was responsible for the whole district. Hurram was in a certain sense Devi Sinha's nominee and representative, and acted by fixed instructions contained in a document entitled Wajebad Aruz. On this point Devi Sinha said: "If Hurram has acted contrary to my orders, signified to him upon this Wajebad Aruz, he is the person who should be responsible." And the official conclusion was that, "from the substance of the Wajebad Aruz and the tenor of Devi Singh's answers, there is reason to believe that he was considered both by Devi Singh and himself as the collector of Rungpore, acting under Devi Singh's orders, independent of the zemindars."

With regard to Hurram, the report goes on to allege that some time after these incidents, and, indeed, whilst they were being considered, "the zemindars in 1189 complained to Devi Singh against Hurram for exactions and oppressions during the time he held the management of the collections. He referred their complaints to arbitrators, who made an award finding Hurram guilty of having exacted a part of the sum complained of, acquitting him of another part, and leaving yet another part undecided. It was also alleged that Hurram had employed violence and threats, but this information does not appear to have been given on oath."

To this general charge Devi Sinha's reply was that "Hurram had the sole management of the collections of the district during the year, and that he did not interfere in the business." And upon further inquiry the Committee found "that Rajah Devi Singh actually resided in Dinajpore the whole or the greater part of the year 1188, at which distance it would have been difficult for him to attend so closely to the conduct of Hurram and his officers in Rungpore as to restrain them from acts of oppression, which can only be effected by a local control. We must also observe that the proofs of these charges, although capable of clear and direct evidence, have not been laid before us."

Coming next to the disturbances and their origin, the Committee wrote:

"The Muchulka of Sheik Mahomed Mullah, Collector of Carjeehaut, in which he says, according to the former plan and papers, he collected, in conjunction with the zemindars, the tax of Dereenwillah. It does not appear that Mr. Paterson examined evidence to prove the authority of the two former papers, and Sheik Mahomed Mullah denied upon oath before the Committee that he collected those taxes. From his examination it appears that, when he was deputed Sezawul, Rajah Devi Singh gave him an account, stating the whole of the remaining demand against Carjeehaut for the year, and ordered him to collect it; and being asked if these two articles were included in the gross amount, he said he did not know; that the zemindars were at this time in Rungpore under peons, and that two of them, Rameaunt and Sham Chowdry, went with him to the Mofussil; that he kept peons (Mohussils) over them, in which state they continued until the insurrection broke out. And yet he swears that the zemindars did everything.

"The evidence of this man, although very evasive and suspicious, destroys the effect of the Muchulka he before delivered. We must here observe that the exaction of Batta and Dereenwillah is what the ryots principally complained of on their first rising. In their answer to Mr. Goodlad's first purwannah they complain of Dereenwillah and an increase on their rents of two annas (Batta),

THE MARBLE SHANASHIN.

Front view of the big temple at Nashipur.

To face page 31.

and that these taxes were the principal cause of the insurrection appears probable from the behaviour of the people."

In further support of the alleged ill-treatment which was resorted to to bring in the taxes, and which was the direct cause of the disturbances, a series of attestations was produced. According to them a Tokedar named Jadoonundun Surmah committed various acts of cruelty, flogging some victims and pulling out the whiskers of others. Mr. Paterson had accepted these statements with absolute credulity, and it is rather remarkable to find that the Committee followed his example. Yet in no country in the world was it so easy as in India to fabricate evidence.

Whatever its causes, the following description of the insurrection seems accurate enough:

"With regard to the rise and progress of the insurrection we find that it began in Carjeehaut, Coonkneah, and Tepah about the 7th of Mang. The Collector, on receiving information of it, dispatched the Nazir Gomanee to the ryots in Carjeehaut to know the cause of it; but a little after he sent Lala Manick Chund with a purwannah to the ryots, desiring them to depute, without any apprehension, a part of their number to lay their complaints before him, assuring them of redress. On the other hand, should they continue their depredations, he would send a party of sepoys against them, seize and punish them as thieves and dacoits. The ryots near Calpanny had killed Gourmohun and drove the other Amlah out of the country.

"They received the purwannah with great respect, and on being assured that they would be only required to pay jumma and batta as in 1187, they promised to return to their homes. Meanwhile, Lieutenant Macdonald was coming up at the head of a small force to deal with the ryots if they did not give in. In the belief that the ryots had returned to their homes, the Sezawuls were again sent into the Mofussil. When one of them issued Tallab

Chitties for revenue, three or four thousand ryots assembled and attacked him. Nion Singh, a subahdar, was sent to his assistance. The insurrection spread to other parts of the district, and appeared so formidable to the Collector that he thought it necessary to collect as many barkandazes as he could. Several battles were fought between the ryots and the sepoys. On February 12 the ryots wrote another petition to the Collector, in which they complained that he had not done them justice. He replied that their complaint was false, and that they must pay Batta, and that they must pay Curtennee according to 1187. Hostilities continued until February 22, when a decisive battle was fought and sixty ryots were left dead on the plain. Several were taken prisoners, and an end was put to the disturbances."

The effect of the disturbances was to draw greater attention to the Rungpore situation, and at this point it will be appropriate to give Devi Sinha's replies to the various charges. First, with regard to the alleged sale of talooks in Rungpore he wrote: "My answer respecting the sale of talooks in Rungpore is as follows:

"Out of the sum stated as Wassil amounting to 77,776,13.4 rupees, only 29,220,2.12.3 rupees was received into the Treasury I have said all I know on this head. As to the balance, amounting to 48,556,0.11.4 rupees, this was the sale made by the zemindars of their own free will, and, as is the custom in Rungpore, without the knowledge of the Collector, the Dewan, or the Sudder Mustager. I know not even the names of the sellers. The gentlemen have taken no notice of this, but in their Report to the Council have stated the whole of it to have been received by me. I beg your attention to this.

"RAJAH DEVI SINGH."

Secondly, on the subject of Dereenwillah and the other alleged new taxes, he wrote:

"I have received your purwannah setting forth that the Bundobust of Rungpore for 1190 had arrived under the signature of Mr. Goodlad, from which it appeared that in the year 1188 a tax existed under the head of Dereenwillah amounting to 56,921.3 rupees, and another tax under the head of Woosul Curtennee of 43,427.12.13.2 rupees, and in the year 1189 a tax called Dereenwillah of 37,038.9.6 rupees amounting in all to 1,37,387.8.19.2 rupees, and desiring me to explain these articles, and declare by whose orders they were imposed. Gentlemen, the zemindars received no orders from any person to assess Mahtoots under the heads of Dereenwillah and Curtennee. The zemindars delivered Muchulkas into the Shoristah for 1188 and 1189 to the following purport; that they would collect the afsul, or original rents, with the Aboabs in use in the year 1187, and would not collect any new Mahtoots from the ryots. Several purwannahs issued from the Huzzoor during 1188 and 1189 to the zemindars to the same purport, and the zemindars renewed their Muchulkas upon receipt of the purwannahs.

"All these are forthcoming and shall be produced whenever you please to order them. The following is an explanation of Dereenwillah and Curtennee as far as has come to my knowledge. From the time that the zemindars got possession of the country by engaging for the revenues, they colluded with the ryots, mundals, and patwarries, etc., and lowered the original rents of the ryots, unknown to the Collector, in order to make their zemindaries appear deficient in assets and to conceal the ganjaysh, or profits. To effect this they allowed the ryots deductions under the seven following heads:

1. Delassy Cummee.
2. Buksinda Cummee.
3. Nerikh Cummee.
4. Karijie Cummee.
5. Polotucka Cummee.
6. Mooktah Cummee.
7. Paykasht Cummee.

"Having made false deductions from the Jumma under these heads, they at the time of making a hustabood, or settlement, assessed Mahtoots on the ryots under the heads of Dereenwillah and Russoom Parbonnee, etc., and brought them upon the Jummabundy; and in some instances the patwarries collected Curtennee from the ryots and gave them pottahs at under-rents, unknown to the zemindars. Whenever a measurement was ordered, the ryots objected, and agreed to pay a Mahtoot of one or two annas Dereenwillah to avoid the measurement; and whenever a new collector was sent into the district, the ryots complained of these Mahtoots, representing that they were prohibited, and desiring to pay the revenues agreeably to their pottahs and no more, in this manner laying a foundation for a balance in the revenue. And this practice they have always regularly pursued, receiving deductions with one hand, and paying Mahtoots with the other. The articles stated in the Bundobust alluded to have been in use from Mr. Purling's time to Mr. Bogle's time in 1187. If the accounts of ten or twenty years back are examined, the same custom will be found to have prevailed, which I have fully ascertained; and that also appears from the account Bundobust of 1190.

"Mr. Goodlad transmitted to the Committee such papers as he received from the zemindars. I have authentic accounts, Jummabundy, of one ryot, one monzah, and one purgunnah, for three or four years back, which will prove the chicanery of the zemindars, and shall be delivered when called for. Those papers will justify one person and involve a hundred in guilt.

"Until you thoroughly understand the chicanery of them, in the first place a servant of Government will be ruined, and in the second place the public revenue will decrease yearly, for the reasons already set forth.

"RAJAH DEVI SINGH."

It was at this stage in the question that a material difference of view revealed itself between the two English officials, Mr. Goodlad and Mr. Paterson. Mr. Goodlad supported Devi Sinha; Mr. Paterson accepted the zemindars' and ryots' statements without sufficient examination; and the consequence was that a controversy arose between the two that reflected on the dignity of the service and aroused the ire of the Governor-General in Council. It was under these conditions that the five following Resolutions were passed by the Government, then headed by Warren Hastings. They read:

> "1. That the Committee of Revenue do order that Devi Singh be immediately arrested and confined in the Khalsa for the heavy balance of revenue which he owes to the Company, and more especially as a person accused of the most cruel oppression and extortions.
>
> "2. That the Committee be directed to take proper measures for securing his property, to answer all just demands of the Company, as well as those of the oppressed zemindars and ryots of the districts which he farmed.
>
> "3. That the Committee be informed the Board will appoint a Commission, consisting of three of the Company's servants, to investigate effectually those accusations against Devi Singh and his deputy officers whom Mr. Paterson has reported to the Committee, and which may admit of more determinate and legal proof.
>
> "4. That Mr. Goodlad be ordered immediately to attend the Board to answer certain charges which appear against him in the course of this inquiry.
>
> "5. That a person be appointed to take charge of the Collections and Adawlut till further orders."

For the moment Mr. Paterson's allegations that the zemindars had fled the country and the ryots risen in insurrection through "Rajah Devi Singh's oppressions" were accepted, and Mr. Goodlad's view that "it was all the chicanery of the zemindars" did not find favour. The further inquiry was to find out the truth. For the moment Devi Sinha was the chief sufferer. Here follows his protest against the affront put upon him:

"A Dustuck reciting that I am in balance 3,90,200 and odd rupees, and that I have put many persons to death, having been sent to me with some peons, I have been ordered to be kept in the Khalsa, which order I have without the smallest altercation obeyed, and am now there in the charge of peons. But as I am the servant, the subject of, and obedient in all respects to, the Government, and have never been deficient in any matter, I cannot, therefore, but greatly wonder over the infelicity of my fate that, without my being sent for to the presence, I should, without being made acquainted with or questioned relative either to the matter of the balance or that of the murders, be at once thrown into confinement.

"Wherefore I beg leave to represent if, in respect to the balances outstanding in the country of Rungpore and due from the zemindars, the collection of which was prevented by Mr. Paterson, on what authority I do not presume to determine.

"If, forgiving the zemindars these balances, it being nevertheless your pleasure to exact them from me, why is my credit thus destroyed, and my reputation and character thus injured, since a loss of character to me must inevitably carry along with it every loss to Government, besides that life itself is but a secondary consideration to be devoted to the preservation of one's honour. When things come to this pass, Government will then be no gainers. I am therefore hopeful that, calling me before you, you will first inquire into the merits of my answer delivered on the 20th February relative to the matter of balances, and I make not the least objection to pay whatever may appear justly due from me; for I am not of the profession of a zemindar, and I have heretofore paid towards the Revenue the amount of more than two lakhs of rupees, which I was obliged to acquire for the purpose of taking up the amount on loan. And now also I remain under the shadow of Government, with my life, property, and family at their disposal.

"And if the gentlemen have entertained suspicions of my having put any persons to death, and that my oppressions are to be proved by the declarations of those persons who are in balance, and the very people who have been the causes of all the disturbances (for from such information are the testimonies procured by Mr. Paterson and delivered on by him to the Committee).

"If without inquiry, gentlemen, you should have deemed such productions valid, and have thereupon conceived me guilty of such acts, in resentment for which my confinement has been ordered, I can nevertheless aver and assure you that the facts so charged to my account will never be verified or established; for in truth I have not put to death or murdered so much as a bird, and if any one murder can be proved against me I am ready to make restitution for it with my own person and those of all my family; but until the truth be ascertained I cannot consider it but very opposite to the credit of the gentlemen's Government that I should in the meanwhile suffer without cause.

"Consider also what constraint I have been under for this twelve months past, to have obliged me to repair to Calcutta and to remain here in constant attendance on the gentlemen, whose every order has uniformly met with my ready obedience, and to whom I have never failed regularly to deliver in my answers to the complaints without ever having made use of the smallest evasion or delay, instead of which the present orders have been issued. Besides the English gentlemen I have no other dependence. I therefore rely on their listening to my representations, and passing a just judgment on my conduct."

For the moment, however, Mr. Paterson's personal views—not untinged with sensationalism, for he declared that "thousands of eyes were turned on the Government to see how it would act in this matter"—prevailed over the more sober judgment of the Board of Revenue to the effect that "the proofs hitherto produced of the Rajah's guilt are not sufficiently strong," and Warren Hastings felt bound to appoint a strong Commission of Inquiry. Mr. G. E. Pete, Mr. T. P. Broughton, and Mr. William Douglas were the Commissioners, and Mr. Charles Ogilvie was appointed Secretary.

The instructions to the Commission were set out in a long despatch of thirty-two paragraphs. They were to inquire into the causes of the disturbances, amounting to an insurrection, in Rungpore. They were told that "the insurgents represented them to have been caused by the oppressions and undue exactions of Devi Singh, the Government's farmer, and of his officers; whilst Devi Singh imputed it to an interested desire on the part of the zemindars and ryots to obstruct his realizing from them (more especially as his lease was then drawing to a close) the proper and due revenue." The point submitted to the Commission could not have been put more fairly. Mr. Paterson prejudged the case, assuming Devi Sinha's guilt, and regarding those who held their judgment in suspense as his accessories.

At this juncture Devi Sinha, who was detained in Calcutta while the Commission proceeded to Rungpore, petitioned to be released on his giving security for any amount that he might be called upon to pay. Here follows his petition:

"As at the time of my delivering my first petition to the Honourable Board I was, from the apprehension of losing my honour, altogether distracted, I had not well examined the tenor of the Dustuck, because the peons, coming to me in the night time without my being in the least aware of their approach, waked me from my sleep and carried me to the Khâlsa, where they detained me. I have since taken up a copy of the Dustuck and perceive the term 'murder' is not used in it. The contents are as follows: 'The sum of 3,90,262 rupees 14 annas being due from Rajah Devi Singh, Malzamin of Rungpore, etc., and, moreover, divers oppressions and innovations having been exercised by him on several of the zemindars and ryots of Rungpore, you are therefore deputed agreeable to the orders of the Governor-General and Council, and must seize the said Rajah, confine him in the Khalsa, and by the strictest injunctions get the revenue of Government discharged, and you are to keep the said Rajah in confinement till another order is issued by the Huzzoor.'

"I therefore request, gentlemen, that considering my distracted situation you will be kind enough to excuse my mention of murder, which was inserted by mistake in my petition. To the payment of the balance and the innovations which the Board has charged me with I am ready to answer. In liquidation of the former I will even tender a Malzameen security on this condition: that he shall discharge whatever arrears appear due from me by the Board's investigation, and that they will also cause payment of what shall appear due to me from the zemindars of Rungpore.

"I trust you will condescend to take these my requests into your consideration and release me, and when security has been taken that you will order me to attend the Supreme Council, there to represent my situation,

"RAJAH DEVI SINGH."

As the Indian Government might be in the position of claiming revenue from Devi Sinha orders were given to the Chief of Murshidabad to place a kind of restraint or embargo on his property in that place. It was at first proposed to make a strict inventory of his possessions, but, fortunately, the Revenue authorities, touched by the following appeal, countermanded the worst features of the investigation, and the Governor-General not merely sanctioned the indulgence, but declared that there was no wish that "the reputation of his family should in any degree be injured." This is Devi Sinha's appeal:

"I have just received information from Murshidabad that Mr. Fendall and his Munshi, accompanied by a Khalsa Mohirir and two others belonging to the Canongoes, with several other persons, are gone to my house to take an inventory of my effects. I am apprehensive they will make no exception in favour of those belonging to the women's apartments. Since the receipt of this account I have given myself up to despair, since I cannot possibly survive the disgrace of my family. I am unable to account for this oppressive conduct towards me.

"Allow me to observe that I am of an honourable family, and have never since my arrival in Bengal experienced the like. If any attempt should be made to take an account of the effects in my Zeenannah, my women, perhaps, may be induced to put an end to their existence.

"I myself am ready to give up my life for the Company from whom I have in a manner received it.

"I conjure you, in the name of God, gentlemen, to represent these particulars to the Honourable Board, and to procure suspension of these measures. Otherwise I shall call upon you for redress on the Day of Judgment.

"RAJAH DEVI SINGH."

Before the Commissioners began their work they represented that, in their opinion, Devi Sinha ought to be allowed to appear at their sittings and plead his own case. They pointed out the criticism that would be certain to follow from an attempt to judge and condemn him in his absence. The Government's proposal was that he should appoint a Vakil, and appear by deputy, but the Commissioners replied: "You cannot compel him to appoint one, and if he refuses you are placed in the same invidious

VIEW OF THE PALACE FROM THE EAST.

To face page 44.

position." And this was precisely what happened. He presented the following petition:

"Your Petitioner some time ago solicited your Honourable Board to be allowed to give security, but he has not yet been honoured with a reply. He now understands that out of your great lenity you have appointed three gentlemen, in order to re-examine into the business of Rungpore. In this case an idea occurs to your Petitioner, which he most humbly represents, that if the gentlemen are to inquire into this business upon the spot and your Petitioner remains here in confinement, the representations of his accusers would only be heard without his having an opportunity of defending himself, and render it impossible for your Honourable Board ever to come to the truth. Your Petitioner therefore humbly prays he may be allowed permission to attend the Gentlemen Commissioners on the spot, that being present a proper inquiry may be made into every particular. If this is not admitted of, the same will occur as when Mr. Paterson was there, who, receiving petitions of complaints from the zemindars, whose interest it was to sink (reduce) their balances, and without making any inquiry into them, he brought all this trouble on your Honourable Board and infinite distress to your humble Petitioner. In the present inquiry the future character and life of your Petitioner are concerned. He has no person with him whom he can sufficiently trust, and, indeed, it is a matter of that nature that no proper inquiry can be made unless he is present to answer for himself.

"Your Petitioner therefore most humbly prays he may be permitted to repair to the place of inquiry, and for the satisfaction of the Honourable Board he is ready to give such security as they may deem necessary. Your humble Petitioner is here in Calcutta, and is willing to give any security the Honourable Board may demand.

"The people placed to attach the house and effects of your Petitioner at Moorshedabad are a source of vast distress to your Petitioner's family and relations. He therefore humbly petitions they may be withdrawn, and, as he has served the Honourable Company with fidelity these twenty-five years, hopes this indulgence, after the Honourable Board has taken security, will not be denied him."

This petition produced no immediate effect, and when Rajah Devi Sinha was called upon to nominate a representative, he declined to do so, alleging the very reasons that the Commissioners had conceived he might. Here is his plea:

"I am honoured by the receipt of your purwannah, informing me that it is the order of the Governor-General and Council to depute a Vakil on my behalf to attend the Gentlemen Commissioners of Rungpore, and that I should inform you of his name. I before had the honour to represent to you that I had no person sufficiently acquainted with the particulars of my business as to be competent to answer the allegations of my accusers. Let me entreat you, gentlemen, to consider the peculiar delicacy of my present position. In this inquiry my character, fortune, and perhaps life, are at stake. These are objects not to be entrusted with any agent whatever, even with a brother. The smallest mistake on his part on any questions the gentlemen may please to ask him, and which, from its being impossible that he can be acquainted with all the minutiæ of the circumstances, he may be unable to answer, may tend to my utter destruction. I therefore, gentlemen, most earnestly and humbly petition, on every principle of justice and humanity, that you will take from me such security as you may deem proper for the demands of Government against me, and if personal security should be required from me, I am ready to enter into any engagements you gentlemen may think necessary, or even if it be necessary that you will send a guard with me, and allow me to repair to the place of investigation, that I may have as fair an opportunity of exculpating myself as my accusers have of criminating me.

"I also humbly request that you will write to the Gentlemen Commissioners of Rungpore to conduct their inquiry in the presence of both parties, and in that situation, whatever investigation they may make, it will be impossible for me to object to or complain of my fate when it is founded on a fair and impartial inquiry in the presence of both parties. The trouble and anxiety I have experienced these last fifteen months, and my present disgraceful confinement, have all originated from the former inquiry, entirely consisting of the accusations of my enemies, without my having had any opportunity of being confronted with them, and consequently any means of a fair and impartial vindication.

"If the Gentlemen Commissioners of Rungpore are to make an equitable inquiry, how is it possible they can conduct it when one of the parties is not present to defend himself? You, gentlemen, must well know that a person may assert falsities of another in his absence which are too palpable to urge when he is present. Witnesses may be brought to allege things the falsity of which, by my being present, might be immediately detected, and which otherwise must stand as incontrovertible proof against me. Let me entreat you, gentlemen, not to construe my objection to sending a vakeel into a mark of disobedience to your orders. Could you, gentlemen, form an adequate idea of my present situation, I am sure your humanity would lead you to pity the cruelty of my case.

"My accusers are on the spot; they are zemindars. They are indebted to me near four lakhs of rupees, to avoid the payment of which it is evidently their interest to criminate me as much as they possibly can. They possess unbounded authority over their country and vassals, and consequently have every advantage against me. It is therefore utterly impossible I can defend myself with the partial knowledge of a vakeel. I do therefore, gentlemen, again humbly entreat you that you will attend to this my representation, and allow me to repair to Rungpore, that, by having an opportunity of defending my conduct, I may be able to wipe away the load of suspicion and virulent accusations which I now labour under, and convince you that your Petitioner is not unworthy of your countenance and support."

This petition was referred to the Commission of Inquiry, and the following reply was sent by it to the Government:

"When we consider the variety and nature of the charges alleged against Rajah Devi Singh, and how deeply our characters are engaged in the clear and impartial investigation into the proof of these, we apprehend an effectual inquiry cannot be made into the several charges against the Rajah, unless he is permitted to attend this investigation in person. We further apprehend, if the Rajah is not permitted to attend this investigation in person, he will protest against this Commission, and that such a protest would invalidate the acts of the Commission."

In consequence of this prudent advice the Government gave way, and decided that if Rajah Devi Sinha paid up the balance claimed against him he should be allowed to go "under a proper and sufficient guard" to Rungpore to be placed at the disposition of the Commissioners. But the condition imposed, involving the payment of a sum of 3,90,262 rupees (nearly £40,000 at the currency of the day), was too hard and impossible of fulfilment. It drew forth the following further and very characteristic petition from the accused Rajah:

"Your Petitioner is honoured by the receipt of two purwannahs from the Committee conveying the commands of the Supreme Council—the other informing him that the Honourable the Governor-General and Council had thought proper to direct that he should pay the balance of

3,90,262 rupees, his claim on account of the Tahoda, should be afterwards heard, and he should be sent under charge of a guard of sepoys to attend the Commissioners.

"From the contents of the purwannah, your Petitioner understands it is not the pleasure of your Honourable Board to receive security pending the suit, but require the sum of 3,90,262 rupees in ready money, and it may probably happen on an adjustment of the account that so much is not due; the attachment of your Petitioner's property is not taken off, and he is to be sent a prisoner to Rungpore.

"By these orders your Petitioner is overwhelmed by a river of grief and affliction, for as he to the best of his power and abilities had contributed to the interest of the sirkar, and by the strictest integrity in the discharge of his duty, including the province of Dinajepore, he had paid during the two years of his holding the farm an increase of five lakhs upon the revenues of the year 1187, so he hoped that his services would have procured him the good opinion of your Honourable Board and some distinguished marks of your approbation. But the times are adverse to your Petitioner.

"Notwithstanding the misrepresentations of his accusers have brought upon your Petitioner his misfortunes, yet by the grace of God he relies on the justice and humanity of your Honourable Board that a full inquiry will be made into the truth or falsehood of the charges against him. For example, ever yielding to this persuasion, your Petitioner, though his accusers were not present, attended of his own accord at the Presidency for a period of fourteen or fifteen months. He incontinently replied to all questions which were put to him, so that by the grace of God not any of the charges exhibited against your Petitioner has hitherto been proved. Three Commissioners have in consequence been appointed to make a full investigation into the complaint, and as yet they have not reported any adjustment of accounts formed by confronting the accusers with the accused and stating whether your Petitioner is legally indebted or not.

"Your Petitioner humbly begs leave to lay these circumstances before your Honourable Board, and also further to recall to your remembrance the subject of his former petition, and that, as he is also suddenly called upon for a ready-money payment of a very large sum, he hopes your Honourable Board will recur to precedents whether an instance ever occurred under the Company's administration of a man's being called upon for payment while his suit was pending in a court of justice. If in this representation your Petitioner may unintentionally have deviated from the respect due to your Honourable Board, he implores your pardon and entreats you to consider his situation that his future life and honour are all at stake. He speaks with the confidence of conscious innocence, and of his inability to perform what is required of him, and therefore humbly submits to the consideration of your Honourable Board the various difficulties, losses, and distresses to which he is exposed by his present situation. A summary of these are hereunder stated:

"1. Whenever your Petitioner's account shall be adjusted, it will thereby appear that he is not indebted to Government in the sum required of him. But suppose a case, that a balance was justly due from any individual, would it not be a most difficult matter for that individual to furnish in ready money a very large sum upon credit from any responsible shroff? How is it possible for your Petitioner to do it, deprived of all his employments, and dismissed as he has been for sixteen months past, and when not a pice of the property of the sirkar is in his hands? He lost considerably by his farm. By coming to Calcutta he is put to extraordinary and heavy expenses. He is a prisoner in the Khalsa, though no crime has been proved against him. His goods and effects are attached, his credit ruined with men of all sorts, and he is in his own person degraded. Reflect upon these circumstances, whether it is possible for a person so situated to furnish so very considerable a sum? Upon the hope, indeed, of being enlarged from prison, and the withdrawing of the attachment on your Petitioner's effects, he might by solicitations and importunities to such of his friends and acquaintances as are men of credit obtain their consent to become security upon the following conditions, that they should be responsible for the monies indisputably due to Government agreeable to an investigation to be made by the Commissioners. Your Petitioner is ready to pay any sum justly due from him, and hopes your Honourable Board will attend to his prayer and his petition.

"2. Orders have been issued that your Petitioner's claim for the remaining term of Tahoda should be hereafter considered. The case is as follows: His claim amounts to above four lakhs of rupees due to him, agreeable to authentic documents, from the zemindars and farmers of Rungpore. They not having paid this sum, to evade it, therefore, they caused commotions and troubles in the country. For instance, Gourmohun and Goculmattah and other farmers and servants of credit acting under the Sudder farm were killed in the insurrection, and your Petitioner's cutchery was plundered and set fire to, and confusion and murder ensued in all parts of the Mofussil. Mr. Goodlad, being informed of these tumults, employed himself so effectually to suppress them that peace was once more restored, and ten or twelve thousand rupees of the collection were duly brought in. In the meantime, Mr. Paterson, being arrived at Rungpore, made no investigation (I am ignorant with what orders for his presence) into the cause of these commotions, but, taking the insurgents under his protection, occasioned the loss of the whole balance to the Government, and, having composed a paper of particulars, threw aside the account of balances, and wrote to the prisoner that there was nothing in the Mofussil due to the

Sudder farmer, and beside framed an accusation imputing that the said farmer had collected more than his right. In this predicament, after the arrival of that gentleman, not one rupee was collected, and orders were besides sent from the presence to Mr. Goodlad that the revenue of the tobacco and poppy harvests, upon whose resources depend the whole weight of the collections of Rungpore, should be put off to the next season, and that the farmer should not be permitted to collect them up to the end of the month of Cheit, at which period his lease would cease. As he was by these means deprived of the opportunity of making his collections, how then can the conditions of his cabooleat and pettah, according to the usage in such cases, possibly be considered in force? Commissioners are now upon the spot, and might inquire into all these particulars by confronting of the accusers with the accused. The truth or falsehood of your Petitioner's representations would be easily ascertained, for which he most anxiously wishes and entreats your Honourable Board would be pleased to direct the Commissioners to inquire whether such balances are actually due to him or not.

"Your Petitioner prays that in the same manner as during these fifteen months of the pendence of the inquiry your Honourable Board did not demand of him the payment of the balance, but considered the inquiry as necessary to direct a decision on it, so now also, when this inquiry may be the last and soon finally settled, you would not press your Petitioner, that you will be pleased to wait until the conclusion of the inquiry, and to the sum ascertained your Petitioner can have no plea to offer for delay of payment.

"3. Your Petitioner formerly requested that your Honourable Board would take sufficient security from him for the claim of Government, or permit him in person to go under a guard to the place of investigation. He now again requests that, if you do not consent to take security, he may be sent under a guard, hoping it would not be deemed improper or disrespectful in him to stipulate that no injury be offered to his honour. As your Honourable Board are just and generous, and your Petitioner, from his peculiar hard fate, is fallen into multiplied distresses and difficulties, and the inquiry is now passing, he hopes that you will hear with attention and compassion these three separate articles of his Petition, and give orders, conformably to your wisdom, that the inquiry may be carried on with such impartiality that he may not fall a sacrifice to the malice of his enemies and the sirkar not suffer loss."

This petition was taken into formal consideration by the Council, and, although exception was taken to its tone, especially in the reference to Mr. Paterson, a decision was made in favour of Devi Sinha with regard to the substance. It was admitted that it would be rather unjust to call upon him to furnish ready-money at a moment when his property was under distraint, and when he had been kept in confinement for some twelve months or more. It was also recognized that the view of the Commissioners as to his presence being indispensable could not be ignored. On both these grounds, then, it was decided that Devi Sinha might furnish security for his liabilities. Two sound sureties were forthcoming in the persons of Cossinant Baboo and Gerdher Saw.

Before he passed under the control of the Commission, he was asked to explain how it was that Dereenwillah, etc., was established in Rungpore in 1188 and 1189. He replied that he had *never* authorized it; that, on the contrary, he had done everything to prevent it; and explained that it had arisen from a collusive transaction of the zemindars, who, in order to appropriate themselves part of the public revenue, lowered the rents of the ryots, while at the same time they clandestinely assessed upon them a Dereenwillah equal to the amount of the apparent reduction.

As a great deal of the case conjured up by Mr. Paterson's overheated imagination turned on the way in which signatures were obtained to the original agreement with the ryots, the clear evidence of one Praun Roy, a local leader, becomes of importance. After reading it, it will have become quite clear how easily Mr. Paterson was misled by the fact that some of the signatures of the Muchulka had not been appended by the signatories themselves:

"Praun Roy in his examination deposes that, on the complaint of the ryots to Mr. Goodlad regarding Dereenwillah and Batta, the complaint was referred to the arbitration of Lalla Manick Chund, who settled the demand of Dereenwillah, etc.; that he (Praun Roy) told the ryots to give an agreement to that effect; that some ryots remained and signed the agreement; that some went away and did not sign it; that the old ryots, who received deductions from 1187, were satisfied; that the new ryots, who received no deductions, were not satisfied. That after the agreement was signed he went with some ryots and gave the agreement to Rajah Devi Sinha, and told the Rajah that the ryots agreed to pay two annas Dereenwillah, etc., and had given an agreement to that purport, after which the Rajah gave the ryots betel and dismissed them. The ryots who were not satisfied did not return to their houses."

At this stage of the question Mr. Paterson's part in the affair deserves notice. He was shown Devi Sinha's latest petition, and after reading it he penned a very angry reply, in which, after alleging that "the Rajah made sundry charges against him," he styled him "an artful and designing delinquent." But he did not confine himself to attacking the unfortunate Devi. He rated his own Government in the following sentence: "Instead of being supported as the officer of the Government, the whole artillery of accusation is turned against me by my very employers." The Government seem to have been quite frightened by Mr. Paterson's strenuous language and by his confident assertion that "not an Englishman, not a native, does not believe in his heart of the existence of these oppressions and of Devi Singh's guilt." His peroration reads: "Can the supporters of this man, then, hope to screen his delinquency behind any want of formality in me? Or will any error of mine convince the world of his innocence?" In 1784 the representatives of the East India Company had not become accustomed to appeals to the world at large and the general public conscience. As the best way out of the difficulty, it was decided that Mr. Paterson should be allowed to go to Rungpore, with exceptional rights in calling witnesses and controlling the evidence. In this way, Warren Hastings and his Council imagined that they had got rid of a nuisance. They were mistaken, for humouring Mr. Paterson could only be accomplished by treading on other people's toes. In plain words, the Supreme Government had reckoned without its own special Commission.

CHAPTER IV

THE CHARGES AGAINST DEVI SINHA (*continued*)

When the Commissioners at Rungpore heard of Mr. Paterson's intrusion on their domain, they wrote a very dignified protest, and backed it up by a formal declaration that they would adjourn their sittings until they received satisfaction. They wrote: "We would only remark that his (Paterson's) request implies a severe insinuation against the members of this Commission, a violent prejudice against Rajah Devi Singh, and a disposition but ill-calculated to ensure a cool and impartial inquiry into circumstances of so serious and solemn a nature." They were not less emphatic with regard to the Board: "Mr. Paterson's being allowed to attend, to call witnesses and take notes is a grave reflection on the dignity of the Commission," and they then called upon the Board to revoke his appointment and meantime suspended their own sittings.

The Board had no choice but to comply. It humbly explained its motives in giving Mr. Paterson leave to proceed to Rungpore, and left the Commission its full liberty to hear him or not as it liked. The Commissioners replied by saying that they were satisfied, and that they would give Mr. Paterson the chance of not unduly interfering with their proceedings.

Mr. Paterson had fallen foul not only of the Commission but also of the Committee of Revenue, which only took notice of his attack because "if it were treated with silent

THE NASHIPUR RAJ PRASAD.

To face page 56.

He received visits from the zemindars, and was presented with nuzzer by them, which he touched. He also received a visit from Hurram, one of the principal witnesses against Devi Sinha, and in his case not merely touched but took his nuzzer. These highly improper proceedings were denounced by the Commissioners, who pointed out to Mr. Paterson that "these compliments are due only to persons of the highest power and station." Mr. Paterson's answer was that he would reply to this charge and vindicate his own character when the Commission had decided whether he was to have "the indulgence granted by the Honourable Board at first in its fullest force."

On second thoughts, however, he conceived it might be wiser to make an attempt to mollify the indignation of the Commissioners, and he sent them a long letter beginning with a disclaimer of any intention to reflect on "their integrity and capacity." But there was no change in the tone of his remarks about Devi Sinha, whom he denounced as "a man whose great abilities for every species of intrigue and chicanery are notorious to a proverb." In other words, Mr. Paterson, without waiting for the Commission to investigate the matter, pronounced Devi Sinha guilty, and those who declined to decide until they had examined the evidence were denounced by him as his abetters. Mr. Paterson was apparently afflicted with the *cacoëthes scribendi*, and allowed his pen to run away with him, for his concluding remarks on the procedure of the Commissioners were as offensive as they well could be, and ill-calculated to secure his ends. He justified his receiving the deputation in a passage that clearly reveals the manner of man he was :

"I duly declare that I see no impropriety in my admitting the compliment of a visit from the zemindars and Hurram after the holidays; it was a duty they owed me for having freed them from the most grievous oppressions that ever were heard of in any part of the world. You seem apprehensive of my influence; it is the highest compliment you can pay me. It is declaring to the whole world the propriety and justice of my conduct."

Mr. Paterson was a notoriety-seeker, a phenomenon in the India of the eighteenth century.

He concluded his letter with a further attack on the Commission for allowing Devi Sinha certain privileges incompatible with "the various and high crimes for which he is arraigned." These were—

1. Allowing him to be attended by a suite of chubdars, subahdars, etc.

2. Because his guard of sepoys did not fix bayonets.

3. Allowing him to have a chair and be seated at the same table as the Commissioners.

The answer to these allegations is best given by Devi Sinha himself, but before quoting his rebutting statement it may be as well to say that the Commissioners' reply to Mr. Paterson was that "it makes any further correspondence on our part with you unnecessary."

Here follows Devi Sinha's petition not to be deprived of his fair privileges:

"The Commissioners at Rungpore have lately informed me that, in consequence of a letter addressed by Mr. Paterson to the Governor-General and Council, they have been pleased to issue an order to the following purport: 'That, understanding that at Devi Singh's interview with the Commissioners on his arrival at Rungpore, they embraced him and permitted him during his examination to sit down at the same table with them, and to go about with a sawarru of chubdars and subahdars, he is, therefore, ordered to give answers, standing, to such questions as may be proposed to him; for, as Devi Singh is accused of having exercised many oppressions on the country, it is necessary he should appear to the natives to be treated conformably to the customs of a Court of Justice.'

"The Governor-General and Council are well acquainted with the hatred Mr. Paterson bears me, which alone has induced him to procure this order, as I never have sat down at the same table with the Commissioners as above alleged; but when the gentlemen are assembled they allow me a chair at the distance of three or four cubits, where the vakeels of the zemindars are stationed, that, being confronted with them, I may appear in the light of a delinquent. Whenever I am called upon I go up to the table and answer whatever questions the gentlemen propose, or deliver in whatever papers they may have occasion for, after which I retire and seat myself at a distance as before. Whenever I am summoned before the Commissioners I am accompanied by four or five hircarrahs, chubdars, and subahdars, etc., to the number of nine men, and am attended by a guard of sepoys; and this is what Mr. Paterson has called going about in a large sawarru. I beg leave to suggest that since I have always been allowed to sit as above mentioned, should I now be deprived of this indulgence it would be the means of degrading me very much in the eyes of my accusers, who would imagine that the Governor-General and Council were incensed against me. The investigation is carried on where the authority of my accusers is in its full force, and where I stand alone against the united efforts of numbers, divested of all power, and confined under a guard. This inquiry, which may affect my property and life, is of so delicate a nature that any variation in the mode of conducting it may render it difficult to distinguish right and wrong. I therefore request that if it should appear on further inquiry that I have not seated myself at the same table as the Commissioners, but, according to their permission, sat at three or four cubits distant from it, and that I have never been attended by more than a few hircarrahs and always under a guard, I may be allowed the indulgence of sitting as formerly, for, should it be withdrawn, it would be a great hardship to be obliged to stand, as the Commissioners often sit till twelve or three o'clock in the afternoon."

There is a colloquial saying, "Throw mud and some of it will stick." The Supreme Council had been impressed by Mr. Paterson's assertion that a certain state and freedom had been allowed to Devi Sinha, and, while answering Paterson, called upon the Commissioners to furnish an explanation. The Commission sent in Devi Sinha's petition just quoted. The Supreme Council passed the following censure on Mr. Paterson for his attack on the Board of Revenue at the same time that they gave him permission to return to the Presidency:

"Ordered that the Board's displeasure be expressed to Mr. Paterson at the acrimonious terms used by him to the Committee of Revenue; and he be informed, if he means by these expressions to charge the members of the Committee with having wilfully misrepresented and suppressed his reports, the Board must, in justice to the Committee, call upon him to produce the proof of so severe a charge, but at all costs censure him for making use of such reflections."

It is not very easy to follow the causes of the moderation of the Council in dealing with the impertinences of Mr. Paterson, and we cannot feel sure whether it was influenced by the desire to give him rope enough to hang himself or by fear of his creating a scandal at home. The Council would have been wiser in its own interests and certainly in those of Warren Hastings to have smashed Paterson at once as a venomous fly.

The following explanation, given by the Commissioners as to their reception of Devi Sinha, is not without its amusing side, and deserves to be quoted:

"On the day of the Rajah's arrival he came to Mr. Pete's house, and being under no restraint from his guards he passed through the hall, and unexpectedly ran into a private room where Mr. Pete and Mr. Douglas were sitting, and embraced them, and sat with them at the table. On his next attendance, the Rajah was sitting in the hall, and, upon Mr. Pete's entrance into the hall, the Rajah suddenly ran up to him and embraced him, and also embraced Mr.

Douglas, who followed Mr. Pete, and seated himself at the table with the Commission.

"The Commissioners in their situation were sensible of the impropriety of admitting the Rajah's embrace and suffering him to sit at the table with them, and the next time, when he advanced to embrace them, declined it and ordered him to his chair. On his sitting down the Rajah attempted to draw his chair near the table, but the Commissioners forbid him, and ordered him to sit further back to the distance of about six feet from the table."

Notwithstanding these admissions that, perhaps, too much liberty had been asserted by Devi Sinha in the first place, the Commissioners adhered to their ground that he was still, pending a verdict of guilty, entitled to the emblems of his rank, and that he ought not to be subjected to the indignity of an escort with fixed bayonets.

The Council, being anxious to get the inquiry over, asked the Commission to fix an approximate date for the conclusion of their labours, and in December, 1784, the Commission replied that they saw no reason why they should not report by April, 1785.

At this stage, reference may be made to the important evidence supplied by Mr. Goodlad. It is especially interesting in showing how and why Mr. Paterson had gone astray in the reading of the facts and evidence at the beginning of the controversy. Mr. Goodlad, it will be remembered, was not merely incriminated by Mr. Paterson's attacks, but suspended from office pending a final decision on the case. During all the preliminary stages of the affair he had been refused a hearing, but at last, in November, 1784, he was allowed to send in his formal replies to the charges. It is unnecessary to quote any part except that bearing on the main issues. He begins:

"It was with infinite concern I perceived that uncommon pains had been used to propagate and establish a belief that Rajah Devi Singh had been guilty of the most shocking crimes; that every possible attempt had been made to raise the passions and arm the prejudices against him; that the accusation had been supplied by invention, and declarations had been substituted for proof; and that the alleged notoriety of the crimes was supposed sufficient to supersede the necessity of further evidence, although those crimes were of the deepest die (*sic*), and of a nature to admit of positive and specific proof. But the investigation of these charges is now referred to a more impartial tribunal, and I leave Devi Singh to his acquittal or condemnation, remarking only that nothing appears to me more contrary to the principles of humanity and to the fundamental laws of justice than to influence the public voice to prejudge and condemn him whilst under trial."

One of the charges against Devi Sinha was that he had put a zemindar in confinement. Mr. Goodlad affirms: "It was I, not Rajah Devi Singh, who ordered the zemindar into confinement upon the clearest proof of delinquency. . . . It is still less probable that Rajah Devi Singh would have avowedly confined a zemindar, particularly at such a period, for exciting ryots to complain of an exaction that had been positively forbidden, and which had been alleged as one of the pleas for the insurrection. It is not probable that Devi Singh would have offered such an insult to me and my authority. These remarks, independent of the explanations given, might be deemed a refutation of the charges. Permit me further to observe that it was upon the grounds of this accusation, transmitted by Mr. Paterson in general terms to the Committee of Revenue, that they authorized him to put Rajah Devi Singh into confinement, and upon proof declared that they would order him down to Calcutta; that I know of no proof that has been exhibited by Mr. Paterson in support of this charge, that I never heard he had made any inquiry into it, and that I believed it to depend on the bare assertion of the zemindar, and that I conceive it was Mr. Paterson's duty to have made the fullest inquiry into this charge before he stated it as the ground of an accusation of Rajah Devi Singh, and of an attack upon my character."

With regard to the charge that the Rajah had forced the

zemindars to sign unfair agreements, the following is conclusive:

"I called on the farmer (*i.e.*, Rajah Devi Singh) for his engagements with the zemindars, and when I had obtained them I called upon each zemindar separately to know if his engagement was of his own free will. On the engagement being admitted valid, I put the initials of my name to it, as I always do to any Persian or Bengal paper that I examine, for the purpose of preventing the change of it and as a memorandum that it has undergone examination. ——— said he was not responsible for the balance, as Rajah Devi Singh had attached the Mehal by sending his own people to make the collections. I asked him if at the time the Mehal was attached there was any balance. He said 'Yes.' I sent for the Jumma Wasil Backey and found it to be a sum of not less than 58,000 rupees. I told him that Rajah Devi Singh had an undoubted right, agreeable to standing usage all over the country, to attach the Mehal on a balance being incurred, and that this plea would not exempt the zemindars from being answerable for whatever balance might remain at the end of the year. The answer Gungarrain made me was particularly insolent, and I ordered him to be turned out of the cutchery, and should have deemed myself justified in inflicting a further punishment upon him which his conduct merited."

Mr. Paterson alleged that the insurrection was due to Mr. Goodlad's orders to Lieutenant MacDonald. Mr. Goodlad rejoins:

"It is impossible you can form any adequate idea of the violence of the insurgents. I had hourly reason with every other inhabitant of Rungpore to apprehend that the Public Treasury, the town of Rungpore, and the Company's factory, would be attacked and plundered, and we were under the necessity of taking measures for our defence. In such a situation I presume necessity would justify the orders I gave to Lieutenant MacDonald. . . .

"The conclusion of this charge is that, in consequence of my orders, a busneah was hung. . . . No busneah was ever hung. Lieutenant MacDonald apprehended a spy, who was executed."

Finally, on the point of his having shown undue favour and partiality to Rajah Devi Sinha by employing his brother Bahadur Sinha, Mr. Goodlad wrote:

"Mr. Paterson asserts that I brought up with me to Rungpore Bahadur Singh, Rajah Devi Singh's brother, that I threw the district into the hands of many of the Rajah's officers, etc. To this accusation, dictated in the same spirit and with equal truth with many others, I shall reply by facts. I deny that the district was given to Devi Singh's officers; the whole of it, except ——, was leased to the zemindars. I arrived at Rungpore on June 5, and Bahadur Singh on the 10th of the same month. The next day, the 11th, he again left Rungpore by my order, and never returned afterwards. Mr. Paterson had, it is to be presumed, finished his investigations before Bahadur Singh arrived, as on June 11, the very day the man left Rungpore by my orders, Mr. Paterson despatched his second report on the disturbance to the Committee and requested leave to return.

"If Bahadur Singh's arrival could for a moment have impressed the ryots with an idea of Devi Singh's return, his departure within twenty-four hours after his arrival must instantly have removed that impression. It could not affect Mr. Paterson's investigation, because his request to return fully proves that he deemed it completed."

The Governor-General's Council came to the conclusion that Mr. Goodlad had practically cleared himself from Mr. Paterson's charges.

Mr. Macpherson said: "I think Mr. Goodlad's defence upon each and all of the charges strongly in his favour, but before a final judgment can be passed on each charge or upon the whole case we should wait for the issue of the Commission."

Warren Hastings went further: "I entirely acquit Mr. Goodlad of all the charges; he has disproved them. It was the duty of the accuser to prove them. Whatever crimes may be established against Rajah Devi Singh, it does not follow that Mr. Goodlad was responsible for them."

But the exculpation of Mr. Goodlad carried with it the disproof of much of the evidence on which the charges made against the Rajah were based.

To return to the Commission, which, fully conscious of the momentous nature of its task, was proceeding in its investigations with due deliberation. The delay in receiving its report began to irritate the Government, and it fixed a time limit for its existence. This, as a final act of grace, was extended for one month, which would expire in May, 1785. In the meantime a succession of disclosures had put the Commission on the true track of the origin of the insurrection. The ringleader, Deijenarrain, the self-styled nabob of the insurgents, was secured, and after a brief incarceration offered to tell all he knew. Before making a clean breast of it he asked what he might expect. But before the truth could be got at there was to be a deal of cross-swearing, and Deijenarrain, anxious only to save his life, was willing to swear whichever way was the more profitable for himself. At one moment he was willing to turn on the zemindars; at another he insinuated that Devi Sinha had so far taken him into his confidence as to inform him that he had bribed the Commission for 96,000 rupees. The most extraordinary feature of the case was that this really ridiculous evidence by a man trying to save his own life should receive the slightest consideration.

The new charges that were introduced by this witness and others supporting him, for similar motives of self-interest, entailed so much fresh inquiry that the main issues became overclouded, and at last the extreme limit of time conceded by the Government ran out, and the Commission returned to Calcutta. They returned with a vague charge hanging over their own heads of having

THE RAJ RESIDENTIAL QUARTERS.

To face page 66.

succumbed to the temptation of a bribe of 96,000 rupees from Devi Sinha.

Their first request was to ask the Council "to adopt those measures which may be most effectual to bring this charge to the proof. We, as members of this Commission, expect and desire no limits or indulgence if this charge should be proved against us in the smallest degree. On the contrary, if the charge is proved, we require that we may be dismissed from the service and branded with infamy, as men guilty of perjury and the basest corruption." At the same time, Rajah Devi Sinha was again brought down to Calcutta, so that the final scene shifts to the capital.

The consequence of this charge of corruption, in support of which it was alleged that Mr. Paterson had given his connivance—for Deijenarrain's depositions had been made to him—was that the Commissioners declined to make any report until their characters had been cleared. The Council, alarmed at this prospect, summoned all the principal witnesses to Calcutta, including Deijenarrain himself.

With the principals reassembled in Calcutta, the matter enters upon a new phase. Mr. Paterson reappears on the scene with a voluminous collection of so-called affidavits and affirmations, which he had induced Mr. Moore, the magistrate who had succeeded Mr. Goodlad at Rungpore, to attest. He had set the Commission at defiance by making his own inquiry, rallying to his side the zemindars and their followers, and even by converting Deijenarrain himself, despite strong locks and bars, into his tool. In these documents not merely the Rajah but Mr. Goodlad were again charged with their old offences, and much more in fresh and ampler detail. Mr. Goodlad was the first to enter his protest. He had been practically exonerated by the Governor-General's Council, and expected reinstatement to his post. This new or revived attack threatened him with a further postponement of his hopes. He wrote:

"At the time my conduct was referred to the investigation of the Commissioners, and my honour and everything that was dear to me lay at stake, that Mr. Paterson should furtively, with Mr. Moore's assistance and influence, collect *ex parte* evidence against me while I am down in Calcutta, unable in any shape to defend myself, and reserving the delivery of these papers till the moment the Commissioners are ready with their report concerning me, shows a degree of personal enmity that nothing but my respect for your Honourable Board prevents my expatiating on. . . . With regard to Mr. Moore, I conceive that he assumed an illegal authority in taking depositions or in any way interfering with matters which were a subject of inquiry for a tribunal erected under the sanction of your Government, either with respect to Rajah Devi Singh or myself."

The Government then called upon the Commissioners to send in their report without delay so far as it related to the charges exhibited by Mr. Paterson against Mr. Goodlad. The report was sent in on October 29, 1785, and deals with the charges seriatim. Only some of them need engage our attention. The Commissioners were even more indignant with Mr. Paterson than Mr. Goodlad was, for he had encroached on their authority. They wrote:

"We think it our duty to declare that we know not by what authority Mr. Paterson did make his examination and take depositions from the zemindars in the presence of Mr. Peter Moore, the magistrate of Rungpore, or by what authority Mr. Moore, as magistrate, could permit Mr. Paterson to make such examination when both the gentlemen well knew that a period had been put to Mr. Paterson's investigation into the cause of the disturbances by the institution of a new Commission, acting under the authority of the Honourable Board."

One of the principal charges against the Rajah was of forcing the zemindars to sign the agreement, and against Mr. Goodlad of having been cognizant of the fact without taking any steps to punish or prevent this pressure. The finding of the Commissioners on the point is important:

"After a very tedious inquiry into the charge, in the progress of which the gomastahs brought their vakeels, mohrus, and all the officers of the zemindars' amlah to prove that their engagements were extorted from them, it did not appear by any proof or consistent evidence that force was used to make the Zemindars give these engagements. On the contrary, it appears, by the depositions of many of the public officers in Rungpore and other responsible men in the district uninterested in the present dispute, that the settlements were not extorted from the zemindars' gomastahs, but made in the usual mode established throughout the country."

In plain words, the Commission decided that there had been no compulsion.

Another of Mr. Paterson's charges was that "from the orders which he (Goodlad) gave numbers of the ryots were put to death, their houses burnt down, and that a man called a busneah, or head of a village, was hung."

The Commissioners' answer to this sensational charge disposes of one of the most prominent incidents in the proceedings:

"We must inform you that at that period the insurgents had assembled, had murdered their amlah, had plundered the cutcherry, were marching through the district in arms, and by threats and intimidation, circulated by their letters through the district addressed to the ryots of several purgunnahs, exciting and compelling the inhabitants of the neighbouring districts to join them, until their numbers had increased to the most alarming degree. Mr. Goodlad issued a purwannah to Mahomed Tukky, a man of respect and consideration, to assemble his people, oppose the insurgents, and assist Lieutenant MacDonald in quelling the insurrection. Mahomed Tukky went after the insurgents, repulsed and dispersed them, and took Nundram and Sufdil, two of their ringleaders, prisoners, and led them through the district, and exposed them with one side of their faces whitened and the other side blackened."

With regard to the financial arrangements for the farm: "The zemindars paid their revenue to Hurram, and Hurram paid the revenue to the Rajah. . . . After a very strict inquiry by the Commissioners, it does not appear that the Rajah himself ever received one rupee on account of the 52,410 rupees which he is charged with by Mr. Paterson. . . . Hurram does not charge the Rajah in his Jumna Wassid with any receipts on account of Seway Rozenamcha, but deposed before the Commissioners that the Rajah never received a rupee on this account. From the above explanation your Honourable Board will be able to decide upon the charge of the difference of accounts between Mr. Paterson and Mr. Goodlad."

With regard to Mr. Paterson's procedure, the report of the Commissioners could not be more emphatic: "Mr. Paterson, in his reply, has not confined himself to the proofs of his charges exhibited against Mr. Goodlad, but by various insinuations and decisions has resumed his inquiry into the Rajah's conduct before Mr. Peter Moore, the Magistrate and Collector of Rungpore, and has passed judgment upon the Rajah even after your Honourable Board had superseded his former inquiry by the appointment of a new Commission to inquire into the conduct of the Rajah at Rungpore.

"By the introduction of these depositions before Mr. Moore, and opposition to the public inquiry carried on by the Commissioners, there existed two Courts in the same district at the same time, making the same inquiry: one by the permission of Mr. Peter Moore, the Magistrate of Rungpore, carried on by Mr. Paterson, the accuser of Mr. Goodlad and the Rajah; the other by a Commission established by the authority of Government. . . . Mr. Peter Moore has not only exercised an extra-judicial authority, but permitted Mr. Paterson to criminate Mr. Goodlad and the Rajah by questions and depositions made before him as Magistrate."

The final paragraph introduces a subject of which more will be heard:

"We shall lay before you the conduct of Mahomed Jaffer, who came up with Mr. Paterson as companion to Rungpore, went from thence to the city, and returned with the office of Darogah to the Faujdarry Adawlut of Rungpore. One of the zemindars, in his petition, lays a charge indirectly against the Rajah, and directly against others in his employ, for robbery and murder, which the zemindar says we never inquired into.

"Information was given us that an inquiry into the murder had been made before the then Darogah of the Faujdarry Adawlut. Upon an application to Mahomed Jaffer, the present Darogah, for copies of the records of the Faujdarry Adawlut regarding the inquiry into the murder, he, under various pretences, delayed the delivery of the records, mutilated with the view to suppression of the only deposition which could exculpate the parties accused, and which it was proved in the Faujdarry Adawlut from a bit of the records delivered over to him when he took charge of the Adawlut."

It is refreshing to turn from the heated language and bitter tongue of Mr. Paterson to the calm reasoning and unimpassioned words of the Rajah in the following statement in his defence:

"The zemindars' gomastahs say if they had not been obliged to make unnecessary expenses they should have paid the money so expended in part of their revenue, and their lands would not have been sold. I acknowledge the truth and propriety of the declaration. But this applies to the zemindars, and not to their gomastahs. The gomastahs had the sole management of the business of the zemindars; therefore it is the interest of the gomastahs of the zemindars to make expenses whether necessary or not for this reason. Why did the gomastahs make their expenses? If it was done by order of Hurram, why did they not complain? If I had refused to have heard their complaints, they might have complained to Mr. Goodlad; if he had refused to hear their complaints, they might have complained at Calcutta. When they did complain to me, I referred their complaints to arbitration."

The Rajah was charged with ill-treating and unmercifully beating an individual named Gungenarain. This is his reply:

"On this day Gungenarain, Gomastah of Shabegpenand, one of the zemindars, has delivered in a deposition that Rajah Devi Singh beat him so much that he remained a whole night senseless and without hope of recovery. Your Commissioners have been pleased to call upon me for my reply to this charge.

"Gungenarain, the gomastah, and ——, although at one time they were granted a deduction of 27,500 rupees, and at another time 31,000 rupees, in lieu of the profits arising from the Huzzooree Mehals, and were allowed to make their own settlement . . . behaved so ill that they never punctually paid up one kist. . . . I received certain information that it was the intention of the zemindars to keep back their revenue for this year, and that they had instigated, therefore, the ryots to rise; that —— had given the signal to assemble the ryots at Kishoregunge and other places, armed with sticks and other weapons of defence . . . had set fire to Kishoregunge cutcherry, plundered the treasure, with the effects belonging to the aumlah of the cutcherry, taken away all the papers, and that the zemindars had absconded themselves and wrote to the ryots urging them on to the murder of Gourmohun. . . .

"When the ryots received the letter of encouragement from the Collector . . . the Collector came down to the cutcherry, which was then held in my house. While he was inquiring into the accounts . . . Gungenarain behaved in a very impudent manner to him, and would not cease although frequently forbid. . . . Gungenarain, upon the Collector's leaving, began to be very abusive, and made use of many improper expressions. . . . I endeavoured to silence Gungenarain, but he could not be prevailed on. It occurred to me that many others might follow the example of this man. . . . In order, therefore, to terrify others, I gave an order that Gungenarain should be beat, but it was not meant to be put in force. When verbal threats, however, had no weight with him and he would not be silent, then I ordered the Neozer to give him a few strokes with a rattan—a kind of punishment practised always over those who are in balance to make them pay their revenue. The peons only gave ten or fifteen strokes with the rattan, and your Commission must know whenever in any part of Bengal or Industan a Soobah or Roy Rozan, or latterly any gentleman, has been entrusted with the collections of the country, that unless some vigour has been exercised the revenue would never have been realised. I had a trust of this nature, and most undoubtedly was so far authorized as to punish such people as retained the Company's revenue or were dilatory in their payments. . . .

"I had nothing to do with the ryots immediately myself. If these people were permitted to breed such disturbances, plunder the country and abscond with impunity, others would follow their example, and I therefore punished Gungenarain. Your Commissioners will be pleased to consider that in this I have done nothing that is not customary. . . . If I shall now be deemed culpable, your Commission will then be pleased to consider that every person and every gentleman who has ever had charge of the collections is also in the same manner culpable with me."

At this stage a fresh and sensational turn was given to

the whole question. In November, 1785, Mr. Paterson produced a man who swore that Mr. Pete had accepted a bill of 70,000 rupees from the Rajah. Mr. Pete and the other members of the Commission called upon the Superior Council to investigate the charge and clear their characters. But before taking up this fresh matter, the Council decided to deal finally with and get rid of Mr. Goodlad's case. It was most anxious to have the Rungpore affair settled, as it had been protracted far beyond its expectations. It examined the whole of the charges against him, and passed Resolutions upon them with the following conclusion:

"Agreed that Mr. Goodlad be informed of these Resolutions, and be made acquainted that the Board consider what he has already suffered during the course of their investigation as a sufficient penalty for that part of his conduct of which they have disapproved, and that he shall be again employed whenever the Board find a proper opportunity for availing themselves of his services."

Deijenarrain, the leader of the ryots, their so-called nabob, had been brought under guard to Calcutta as the man who had started the story that Mr. Pete had received a large sum of money, and that he and his colleagues were "in the power of Rajah Devi Singh." It was as good a tale as could be invented to buttress up Mr. Paterson's charge and to get Deijenarrain out of prison. In the course of his examination he declared:

"Rajah Devi Singh also wrote to me that the gentlemen of the Commission were in his power. I have a copy of his letter to me here, but the *original was lost by the roof of the guard-room at Rungpore falling in.* It had no seal or name to it, but a mark which I understood to be Rajah Devi Singh's."

Deijenarrain's evidence is transparently valueless, and the Council passed a resolution that "it was in no degree direct, and only hearsay." They also pointed out that in the present case there is "no avowed accuser."

After some discussion it was decided to examine such of the persons as could be found among those who had made the allegation to Deijenarrain. At the same time the Commissioners were ordered to send in their report on the Rungpore insurrection without delay. This report consequently was sent in in March, 1786, leaving the charge against Mr. Pete in suspense. It was divided into six parts. We need only quote here those parts which relate specifically to Rajah Devi Sinha. The Commissioners began:

"The importance of the investigation, and the horrid cruelties stated to have been inflicted together with the fullness of our instructions, led and compelled us to make the fullest inquiry, and by every means procure evidence on the charge to vindicate the honour of the Government and the English name, either to disproving such dreadful accusations, or, if proved, bringing the perpetrators of them to punishment."

After this introduction the charges are taken seriatim. The first charge is that "Devi Singh increased the Jumna or rental beyond the ability of the country to bear." On that point the Commissioners restrict themselves to saying that "no such assessment as that laid by Devi Singh was ever levied from the country, and therefore we do not imagine that the country could bear this increase." This verdict is inconclusive and must be taken into account with that on the latter part of the same charge alleging that the Rajah "compelled the zemindars to sign engagements and then confined them."

Many of the zemindars were women and children, and those who were men are described as totally unconversant with business. They were all represented by gomastahs or deputies. It was with them that the Rajah transacted business. A little examination sufficed to show that the alleged confinement consisted in placing peons or mohussils on their estates, but this, added the Commissioners, "is a universal practice throughout Bengal on making a new settlement, especially where a new farmer is appointed."

On the charge of using violence the verdict was: "It does not appear by evidence that the gomastahs were either beaten, or punished, or put in irons, or into confinement, to make them give their engagements, nor by any consistent evidence that any compulsive means were exercised to induce them to give earlier engagements. . . . To which we must add that by the depositions of —— and —— it does not appear that they considered any compulsion had been used to make the zemindars of Rungpore enter into their engagements."

With regard to the employment of sezawuls to make collection on the zemindars' estates—"a usual practice when they fell into arrears"—the Rajah disclaimed any knowledge of the transaction or of the persons appointed to act as sezawuls, and it appears by the deposition of Hurram, delivered April 15, to have been his own act without the knowledge of the Rajah who was at Dinajepore at the time."

The general conclusion of the Commissioners was that no charge of cruelty was brought home to the Rajah, and, indeed, that there was no reason to suspect him of having committed any such acts as were laid to his charge.

The Commissioners went on to explain that no one could be got to take upon themselves the responsibility and risk of getting in the revenue, unless they were invested at the same time with some of the authority of power, adding that the Rungpore zemindars had always had a bad name as delinquents, and had never paid their revenue except under compulsion. Moreover, none of the gomastahs, when called upon to do so, were able to produce proof that their lands seized for arrears of revenue had been sold at an undervalue. In the case of Carjeehaut, when after great pressure and several months delay papers were produced they were found to be estimates, and not the original deeds and account-books. The estimates were also at complete variance with the original complaints of the same people.

On the charge of having purchased some of the lands which the zemindars had to sell in order to make good their arrears of revenue, it was shown that the Rajah had only bought a small portion of them, and that he had always paid a fair price for what he purchased. Moreover, these lands were not bought for personal aggrandizement, but for religious benefactions through his Brahmin family high priest. Under this head the verdict of the Commission reads as follows:

"The prices given for these lands appear to have been very fair; so far from their being sold at an undervalue they were sold at a price very favourable to the zemindars. There does not appear to have been any compulsion in the transaction of the purchase of these lands."

With regard to the charges of cruelty brought against the Rajah, the Commission concluded that "except in the deposition of Govin Mozumdar, and that not supported by any other evidence, it does not appear from any deposition that the Rajah had the least knowledge that such severities were exercised in the districts, or that the zemindars ever complained to him on his arrival at Rungpore during the year of the severities inflicted on them by Hurram. On the contrary, the zemindars and Hurram declared on February 16, 1785, that the Rajah did not interfere in the management of the district for 1188. To Hurram only, then, can the commission of these cruelties be charged."

The Commissioners also found that the Persian translator from the Bengali, relied on by Mr. Paterson, had in several instances magnified trivial acts of no criminality whatever, into crimes of the highest degree. In other cases alterations had been made in the depositions of important witnesses without their knowledge or consent.

We come finally to the admitted cases of cruelty chiefly in Dinajpore and not Rungpore. The distinction is necessary because there was no insurrection in Dinajpore, and also because the evidence showed that the infliction of cruelty for the purpose of collecting revenue from defaulters had long been in vogue in that part of Bengal. Indeed, some of the practices read as if they had been borrowed from "Darkest Africa." On this matter the Commission affirmed:

"It will doubtless appear a matter of surprise as well as of the greatest satisfaction to your Honourable Board to learn that the most dreadful of the cruelties had no existence. But when your Honourable Board shall recollect the mode in which these charges have been brought forward the surprise will cease, particularly when it is considered that the most dreadful charges arose, not from the voluntary complaint of sufferers applying for redress and justice, but from the depositions of —— and ——, men whose misconduct had subjected them either to punishment or apprehension of punishment, and therefore anxious to shelter themselves under a prior accusation.

"We must further remark that the parties subscribing to the complaints were never confronted with the accused, nor can we find that any examination was ever made into the charges subscribed to; therefore a latitude, if not an encouragement for accusation, was given to the ryots without fear of detection of a false complaint, and an opportunity presented to the ryots of evading, or at least of suspending, the payment of the balance justly due to the farmer by a representation of their suffering under such unheard-of cruelties. Hourly experience proves that there is no language of complaint which the natives will not adopt to evade the payment of their revenue."

We come now to that part of the Commission's report which was tantamount to the acquittal of Rajah Devi Sinha:

"When the directions annually given by the Rajah on the settlement, the Rajah's compliance with the requests of the ryots, and the fact that no complaint of the infliction of severities and cruelties was made to the Rajah, are considered, your Honourable Board must decide whether the infliction of such severities was either with his approbation or knowledge, and if such complaint had been made whether he could not, as in the instance of ——, have punished the offenders in proportion to the enormity of the crime.

"Justice obliges us to observe that we have not been able to fix upon the Rajah any knowledge of, or consent to, the infliction of such severities as have been proved, except upon Basdeo Doss and Ramnarrain, who were punished by the order of the Rajah *for their oppression and plunder of the ryots.*"

In conclusion we must briefly sketch the end of the charge made by Mr. Paterson against the Commissioners of having been bribed. When Mr. Paterson, on finding that the matter could not be treated with levity, disclaimed being the accuser, and alleged that he was only the channel of information, the Commissioners very aptly quoted a dictum just expressed by the Attorney-General of the day before Lord Mansfield:

"I did say what common sense dictates, what the law of every civilized state under Heaven prescribes, and there is not a maxim of law to be fetched from any country or age that contradicts, that the man who calumniates and does not accuse deserves to be punished with exemplary severity."

Mr. Paterson was a mere calumniator. The principal object of his wrath was the Rajah, but those who intervened not to protect the Rajah but to ensure justice passed under his displeasure. First it was Mr. Goodlad, but he, more fortunate than the others, was acquitted and restored to his rank and post in eighteen months. Then he fell foul of the Commission itself, accusing Mr. Pete of having taken a bribe of 70,000 rupees, and the whole Commission of accepting 96,000 rupees from the Rajah. If this charge could only have passed current for a brief space, it would have nullified the effect of any decision the Commission might have come to in favour of the Rajah.

Called upon to furnish proof of the serious charge he had brought against the Commissioners, Mr. Paterson had to admit that he had none, and the Council, now presided over by the new Governor-General, Lord Cornwallis, passed the following resolution :

"Ordered that Mr. Pete be acquainted, in answer to his letter, that Mr. Paterson has declared himself unable to support the charge of bribery against the Rungpore Commissioners, of which charge he acknowledged himself, when called on, to be only the channel of conveyance, and that, it being otherwise unaccompanied with any proof, it has been long considered as set aside, and the parties accused to be innocent of the crimes alleged against them."

With regard to Rajah Devi Sinha, no similar decision seems, from the records, ever to have been formally passed ; but the favourable action taken in regard to each of the requests contained in the following petitions show that he was treated as an innocent man against whom the serious charges advanced by Mr. Paterson could not be upheld. This was his first petition :

"I have at different periods had the honour to be employed in the service of the Honourable Company near five-and-twenty years, and faithfully and zealously administered the affairs entrusted to my management. For twelve years that I was dewan of the province of Rajemahl and Purnea I realized sixteen, and never less than fourteen, lacs of rupees per annum, and at the present juncture the same provinces do not yield ten lacs to Government. I had afterwards, during eight years, the honour to hold the station of dewan to the Provincial Council of Moorshedabad, when the revenue was punctually paid, the cultivation improved, and the people satisfied. A reference to the public records and to the testimony of the gentlemen under whose authority I acted will authenticate the truth of the assertion.

"In the Bengal year 1188 I was appointed security and dewan of the provinces of Dinagepore, Rungpore, and Goragaut. This appointment I did not solicit or wish, and in accepting it I conformed entirely to the pleasure of the Honourable the Governor-General, Mr. Hastings, and of Mr. Anderson, the President of the Committee of Revenue. The Committee received engagements from me to pay in two years near nine lacs of rupees increase upon the settlement of the preceding year of 1187. I punctually discharged the revenue of the first year of my lease—1188. The inhabitants were contented, and I had the satisfaction to receive letters from my superiors, highly applauding my good conduct, which letters are ready to be produced.

"In the second year of my lease such abundance of grain was produced as reduced its value in a degree that the sale hardly defrayed the expense of cultivation. Owing to this cause I was prevented from collecting any revenue equal to the amount of my engagements with Government. Nevertheless, impressed with a just sense of attachment to my employers and a regard to my character, I patiently submitted to the loss, and punctually discharged the revenue on account of the provinces of Dinagepore and Goragaut up to the end of Cheit 1189. In consideration of the great plenty of grain, I made large remissions of the rents to the ryots of Rungpore, notwithstanding which they even evaded the payments of the reduced rent and rose in rebellion, excited thereto by the zemindars, in the hope of sinking their balances, as would appear from authentic documents in my possession. Mr. Goodlad transmitted a full account of these transactions to the Committee of Revenue when Mr. Paterson was appointed to investigate the causes of the rebellion, and in the meantime Mr. Goodlad, by his good management and prudence, quelled the rebellion, and the collections, which had suffered a total stop, were again put in train.

"Mr. Paterson, on his arrival, protected the zemindars and ryots, and led them to suppose that they would be granted a remission of their balances, from the hopes of which they were instigated to prefer complaints against me to Mr. Paterson, who proceeded to the investigation of these complaints, and to this end he directed me by letter to cause the attendance of my farmers and of all persons attached to my office, and likewise to furnish my accounts. I obeyed Mr. Paterson's directions, and he confronted me for seven days with the zemindars, their gomastahs, and thousands of other persons, in the presence of Mr. Goodlad, and compared with them my account receipts, and Mr. Paterson delivered me a transcript of my account, so compared, signed by his mutsuddy Kerparam. After this, on the 13th of Bysaack, I proceeded to Calcutta, agreeable to the orders which I had received from the President.

"My account receipts were the only point to which Mr. Paterson directed his inquiries during my residence at Rungpore, but what was my surprise, on arriving at Calcutta, to find that Mr. Paterson had transmitted a number of petitions to the Committee, complaining of my tyranny and oppressions. Mr. Paterson also asserted that no balances were due to me by the zemindars, but, on the contrary, I had collected a sum considerably above my just claims. To such of the complaints as were transmitted to me by the Committee I fully replied. Mr. Paterson remained four or five months after me in Rungpore and Dinagepore, and on his arrival at Calcutta delivered in all the papers respecting complaints preferred against me, but did not adduce a single proof in support of the said complaints. He kept Sheik Mahomed Mullee in confinement, for the purpose of instigating him to asperse my character, and to induce his acquiescence therein he promised his enlargement. I continued in Calcutta, without any further examination being made into my affairs, for above a year. When Mr. Hastings went to Lucknow, and the authority of Government devolved on Messrs. Macpherson and Stubbs, on April 6, 1784, those gentlemen ordered a guard to attach my person.

"The crime for which I suffered this disgrace was unknown to me, none being alleged. Another guard was posted at the same time at my house at Moorshedabad. My effects were sequestrated, and an inventory of them ordered to be taken. . . .

"I afterwards learnt that three Company's servants were appointed Commissioners to proceed to Rungpore, and inquire into the complaint preferred against me, and in consequence thereof I repeatedly presented petitions to the Honourable the Governor-General and Council, requesting that I might attend the Commissioners, and be confronted with my accusers. . . .

"A purwannah was afterwards received by me, dated June 19, 1784, directing me immediately to pay a balance of 8,90,272 rupees, and acquainting me that on the other hand my claims should be adjusted at a future period. To this I replied that the demand surprised me, for, never having had a hearing to ascertain whether it was just or not, disgraced by an attachment of my person, and denied the right of being confronted with my accusers, I did not admit the demands. In my conscience I had not been guilty of any crime, but, on the contrary, had entertained the strongest hopes, by my good conduct, of meriting applause. . . . That the demand of immediate payment of all claims against me, and the postponement of the adjustment of those in my favour, were instances of my ill-fortune. I appealed to their humanity, and solicited that security should be taken, that I might be permitted to attend the Commissioners, under a guard, at Rungpore.

"I received a purwannah in answer, dated June 10, 1784, directing me to give security for whatever balance should be established against me agreeable to the investigations of the Commissioners, and that I should be sent to Rungpore and remain there under a guard while the inquiry lasted. Seeing expostulation vain, helpless, and knowing my presence at Rungpore necessary for my safety, I submitted to the guard as well as the security. . . . I arrived at Rungpore on the 19th of Badon, 1191, when I was informed that the Commissioners had issued a Proclamation requiring the attendance of persons who had complaints to prefer and adduce their proofs, that justice might be rendered. Notwithstanding which, no complainants appeared; and then pikes were despatched by the Commissioners to compel the attendance of witnesses, and the evidence given by the witnesses so compelled would appear in the proceedings not to establish my criminality.

"I suffered various indignities in the course of the trial, for Mr. Paterson obtained an order from the Honourable the Governor-General and Council forbidding that I should be permitted to sit in their presence; thus I underwent disgrace before the proof of my guilt. I was put upon a level with the meanest of the people in a province where a short time before I appeared in a high rank and high power. So situated, encouragement was held forth to complainants, and if guilt had existed the proof of it could not have been concealed.

"These indignities I suffered at a time when circumstances favoured a presumption of my innocence, for the appointment of the Commission was occasioned by Mr. Paterson's having failed in establishing the truth of his accusations, verified by the following extract of the instructions of the Governor-General and Council to the said Commissioners:

"'That Rajah Devi Singh denies the charges made by Mr. Paterson against him for that year, which charges Mr. Paterson has not made good.'

"Other means failing to authenticate the accusation professed against me, the zemindars of Taipa and three or four other persons were instigated to depose before Mr. Moore and Mr. Paterson that I had offered bribes to the complainants not to appear against me. This served to prolong the investigation and distress me, for the Commissioners suspended their proceedings until they examined these depositions, when no proof appeared that I had ever offered bribes.

"Mr. Paterson, after the appointment of the Commissioners, was not invested with any authority, and it was forbid by the Honourable Board that any persons who were parties or witnesses in the cause should hold any communication either with Mr. Paterson or me. Nevertheless, Mr. Paterson, supported by the influence of Mr. Moore, the Collector, privately received and held long conversations with the zemindars and officers of Government at Rungpore. He talked in private with Hurram, my servant. I represented these circumstances in a petition addressed to the Commissioners, offering to adduce the proof; but it was returned to me in a letter under the signature of Mr. Pete as 'highly improper to be received' while the suit was pending.

"Mr. Moore and Mr. Paterson in this manner secretly took the depositions of Durigenarain and others, asserting various matters highly injurious to the character of Mr. Goodlad and me, and carried the said depositions along with them to Calcutta without even communicating the same either to the Commission or to me. I represented their conduct to the Commissioners, urging that the investigation of the complaints rested with them, and that in taking depositions the said gentlemen acted without authority and injured me. I requested that they would inquire into this matter, which they did, and it was found that the depositions above alluded to were secretly taken by Mr. Moore and Mr. Paterson.

"From these facts I conceive myself justified in asserting that circumstances of peculiar hardship have attended my trial, and which I humbly submit to the consideration which it merits when my case comes under decision.

"Persons acquainted with the depositions of the natives of Hindustan will readily be convinced that in my situation complaints of the zemindars might have been easily excited; for, being indebted to me in considerable balance of revenue, and having instigated the ryots to rebellion, to establish criminality against me would be their only hope of evading the payment of those balances and of averting punishment for the murders and other acts of violence committed by them in the course of the rebellion.

"Conformably to the orders of the Honourable Board, when the investigation was completed I proceeded to Calcutta, where I have now resided above one year and a half. During this period I have repeatedly transmitted petitions to Mr. Macpherson, humbly representing that the inquiry into my conduct was now concluded, and, although I had given bail, the guard over my person remained. I earnestly solicited that a decision might pass and the guard be withdrawn. To these representations I never could obtain an answer. I continue in disgrace, to the ruin of my character, separated from my family, and suffering irreparable injury in my fortunes, unable to attend to my private concerns. The extraordinary length to which my sufferings have been protracted is above all vexatious, for it now exceeds five years since my dismissal from office, and I have continued in confinement and disgrace, and in fact have had punishment inflicted, before proof of guilt."

This petition produced no effect, and twelve months later the Rajah repeated it in an abbreviated form, which need not be quoted. Only then did the Council come to a formal decision on the subject:

"The Board, having taken the above petitions into consideration, are of opinion that whilst the cause lies over for decision (which the constant business before the Board may protract to some time longer), every accommodation should be allowed the petitioner which is not inconsistent with the purpose of justice. That they have no reason to apprehend any intention on his part to fly from the event of the trial, which indeed, if he were so disposed, he might effect, notwithstanding the guard now placed over him, with the same facility as if he resided at Moorshedabad. That in whatever manner the trial may terminate, it cannot be denied that the inconveniences stated to be suffered by him are real.

"Resolved, therefore, that the guard of sepoys over his person be withdrawn (October 16, 1787), and that in lieu thereof two persons be appointed from the Khalsa to attend to and watch his movements; that he be permitted to visit his family at Moorshedabad on his engagement to return whenever summoned to make his appearance; and that the bonds of his securities be returned to him on his delivering to the Board of Revenue security to the same amount in certificates, with authority to appropriate the same to the Company's use whenever the orders of the Governor-General in Council may be issued for that purpose."

Thus ended the famous inquiry into the events at Rungpore, and all that can be said in conclusion is that the acquittal of Rajah Devi Sinha, if it lacked the formal decree of a Court or Supreme Council, was complete, for as some alleviation of his sufferings the Government, a few years later, raised his rank from that of Rajah to Maharajah, and conferred upon him many khillats of honour.

CHAPTER V

DEVI SINHA'S SUCCESSORS

Rajah Devi Sinha lived for nearly twenty years after the events described in the last chapter. He had nothing more to do with the farming of the taxes, and he concentrated all his attention on his own affairs. The Mogul Emperor, Shah Alam, had recognized his jaghir as an independent non-tax-paying Raj, and the Indian Government allowed him to prosecute his claims against several of his creditors under his lease as a farmer. One of them, at least, was an Englishman, who eventually had to pay the sum he owed. By this means the Rajah recovered the security he had deposited with the Government for their claims, and his reputation again stood so high among the English officials that the Marquis of Cornwallis conferred upon him the higher title and style of Maharajah Bahadur. On several occasions he was invited to acquire lands, in addition to his hereditary "Raj," in order that the Government might feel sure of receiving its land tax.

The Maharajah, described in the official documents as Zemindar of Hooddah Ekoory, died on April 18, 1805, and as he left no children, his property passed to his brother and that brother's sons.

This brother was Rajah Bahadur Sinha Bahadur, already mentioned. In February, 1779, Warren Hastings had recognized him as Rajah Bahadur. Bahadur Sinha had also served the Indian Government very well, and was at

enjoyed by my ancestors, and that I shall be enabled to live respected and honoured among my peers and equals, and to support the name and rank of my family.

As a token of my attachment and respect, I transmit a sealed bag with a nuzzur of five gold mohurs, which I beg Your Lordship to do me the honour to accept.

To say more would be to transgress the bounds of respect.

The reference in this letter to his responsibility for his father's family and dependents conveyed the idea that he was his heir and representative, and it was on that assumption that Government complied with his request. The language of the official letter is clear and leaves no loophole for misinterpretation. It reads as follows:

To T. Brooke, Esq., Superintendent of Nizamut Affairs at Murshidabad.

SIR,

I am directed to acknowledge the receipt of your despatch of March 13, transmitting a letter from Oodwunt Sing to the Right Honourable the Governor-General's address, accompanied by an offering of five gold mohurs, and stating his solicitude to be distinguished by the title which was enjoyed by his deceased father, the late Rajah Bahadur Sinha.

The British Government has never assumed the privilege of granting titles, but it is at all times ready to acknowledge independent hereditary titles. The title of Rajah, however, has been in the family of Oodwunt Sinha for several generations, and the Governor-General in Council, *supposing that Oodwunt Sinha is the eldest son of the late Bahadur Sinha, and, consequently, the representative of the family*, authorizes him to assume his father's title. As a public acknowledgment of Oodwunt Sinha's new dignity, His Lordship in Council is further pleased to confer on him the distinction of a Khellaut, which, according to the enclosed list, will be transmitted to you through his agent, and on its arrival at Murshidabad you will be pleased to invest Oodwunt Sinha with it on the part of the Government in due form.

I am directed to transmit to you the enclosed letter from the Governor-General to Oodwunt Sinha in reply to his to the address of His Lordship, together with copies of it in the English and Persian languages for your information.

I have, etc.,
J. MONCKTON.

FORT WILLIAM,
August 14, 1812.

Enclosed in Mr. Monckton's letter was the following communication from the Governor-General:

To Rajah Oodwunt Sinha, son of the late Rajah Bahadur Sinha.

I have received your letter announcing the death of your father, the late Rajah Bahadur Sinha, which has occasioned concern in my mind.

I entertain a high sense of your loyalty and attachment towards the British Government, and I consider the nuzzur which accompanied your letter as proof of both; but the acceptance of pecuniary offerings being contrary to the practices of the British Government, I return your offering.

You may be assured that, as long as your conduct is regulated by the principles of fidelity and attachment, you will experience the favour and protection of this Government. As a testimony of my favourable disposition towards you, I have directed Mr. Thomas Brooke, Superintendent of Nizamut affairs, to invest you in my name with a Khellaut on the occasion of your father's decease and of your accession to his title.

J. MONCKTON.

August 14, 1812.

This letter not merely ignored the existence of Kissan Chand, but of his father, Hanumanta, as well.

Rajah Udwant Sinha was undoubtedly a very clever man, and greatly increased the family possessions. The following description of him is taken from a work entitled "Nomenclature of Native Powers and Native Chiefs of India":

"Rajah Oodwunt Sinha Bahadur, son of the famous Devi Sinha (an error for nephew), of Mr. Hastings' time, is a principal person of Murshidabad. He has immense wealth and large commercial dealings, and has besides by purchase at private sales possessed himself of extensive estates in all parts of the country but chiefly at Murshidabad."

Rajah Udwant Sinha enjoyed his honours throughout his life without being disturbed in any way, and he was almost as well known for his religious zeal as for his wealth. He made several pilgrimages to the Baidyanath Temple among other places, and it is curious to read his correspondence with the Governor-General on each of these occasions, and his obtaining permission to travel with two hundred followers, and to be exempt from all customs' duties. In 1816 he removed the Rajbati of his family from Gaisabad, where it had been fixed by his father, to Nashipur (then spelt Naseepore), and he also made large endowments and provided in perpetuity for the attendant Brahmins. The entry on this subject in the Government record is:

"Rajah Oodwunt Sinha, an opulent banker of Murshidabad, got the Governor-General's permission to donate houses and land in Calcutta, and a sum of money, producing together an annual revenue of 24,000 rupees, for the purpose of supporting and maintaining the temple and rites of Raghonath Jee at Nuseepore (Nashipur) the Thacoorbaree of Ruma Bycoonth."

This endowment was quite apart from the enormous cost of the temple itself which is described as a splendid building. The temple is crowned with a central dome sixty feet above the floor, and is ornamented with twenty-five steeples topped with glistening gold minarets which are ninety feet above the base. The shanashin, or arch, is in marble, and there is not a finer or more imposing temple to be found in Bengal. Here he consecrated the presiding deity of the family, Sri Sri Iswar Raghunath Deb Thacoor. In addition he also founded and endowed various minor temples, and he also granted many Brahmatic lands to the Brahmins.

But his charity was not restricted to the Church, and he had the reputation of being a general philanthropist. The following story about him is not uninteresting:

On a certain occasion a poor Brahmin applied to him for help to meet the expenses of his daughter's marriage, which in Bengal is always very great, and sometimes involves the family in ruin. At the first application the Rajah, thinking it adequate for the case, gave him only 5 rupees, but the Brahmin was not at all satisfied with it, and yet he was somewhat at a loss how to induce the Rajah to grant more. But he was at a still greater loss how to defray the enormous cost of giving his daughter a suitably splendid wedding.

Watching his opportunity, he at last saw the Rajah bathing one day in the sacred Bhagirathi, and approaching him hurriedly with clasped hands, he implored him to give him a further contribution of a substantial amount. The Rajah took pity on him, and asked what he wished him to pay, suggesting himself " pachsat san " (five seven hundreds of rupees)? The Brahmin replied " Tathwastee " (so be it). The Rajah, on his return to his residence, ordered the Treasurer to pay him the money.

As a man of business Rajah Udwant Sinha was not merely one of the richest men of his day in India, but he was also an excellent landlord. The zemindars of Bengal were notorious for the bad management of their affairs, and they were always more or less in difficulties. Udwant Sinha introduced an entirely new zemindary system, which is still the model of Bengal. In other words, he succeeded in making the land pay its fair return to the owner and the State. He was thus doubly useful to the Government, for he supported its policy, and he was an example to others.

Udwant Sinha also co-operated with the Government in other ways, and when the local Rajah of Rewah rose in insurrection he was called upon to send his forces to aid the troops operating against him in the following official letter:

The faithless and hostile conduct which the Rajah of Rewah has lately pursued, having dissolved the relation of friendship between the British Government and the Rajah, has compelled the British Government to resort to arms for the security of its rights and interests.

I am satisfied of your disposition to avail yourself of every opportunity of proving your attachment and devotion to the British Government. The object of this Perwana, therefore, is to desire that you will conform to whatever requisitions you may receive from Captain R——, either for the junction of your troops with his detachment for the purpose of being employed in the operations to be undertaken against the Raja of Rewah, or for the continuance of your exertion in defending the passes through your country from any incursions which may be attempted by the Pindarries during the absence of the British troops.

The exertion of your zeal and fidelity on this occasion will confirm the high opinion which I entertain of your character, and will secure to you the especial favour and protection of this Government.

Yours,

J. MONCKTON.

Udwant Sinha took a very considerable interest in foreign affairs, and when news reached India of the exile of Napoleon to Elba, and the conclusion of the long war in Europe, he wrote a letter of congratulation to the Governor-General, to which he received the following reply:

Your letter expressing your great satisfaction at the news of the defeat of the ruler of France and his party at the hands of the victorious heroes and participators of the British Government, and your wish for the health and prosperity of these victorious personages and of the illustrious Government, and containing other good news, and forwarding presents through . . ., has greatly increased my happiness. Whereas you are a well-wisher and favour-seeker of the high and illustrious British Government, consequently the said good news must surely have been the cause of greater satisfaction to you.

The expression of satisfaction and the forwarding of a present, being mere tokens of your good wish, have been the causes of very great satisfaction to me.

I have accepted in mind the present sent, but, according to the custom of this Government, it is remitted.

It is proper that, considering me your constant well-wisher, you should render me satisfaction by writing me your good news. What more shall I write?

G. NUGENT,

October 28, 1814. *General.*

Another instance of this intelligent interest and goodwill was furnished when the Marquis of Hastings brought the Maratha War to a successful issue at the close of the year 1818. The Rajah wrote a letter of congratulation, accompanied by the usual formal present to the Governor-General, and received the following reply:

On receiving the news of my return with victory and peace from my journey to the North-Western Provinces, the letter with the well-wishing present which you have sent expressing your great satisfaction, and containing other expressions of your devoted loyalty, has rendered me great satisfaction. The said news might surely be the cause of greater satisfaction to you, considering the lasting loyalty, esteem, and affection which you have towards this Government.

2. The well-wishing present and the expression of your satisfaction indicate your loyalty, and consequently have become the cause of greater satisfaction to me. The presents sent are accepted and touched, but remitted according to practice. Considering me your constant well-wisher, you should continue to please me by conveying to me the news of your welfare. What more shall I write?

HASTINGS.

February 12, 1819.

Not long after these letters, Rajah Udwant Sinha was taken very ill on one of his numerous pilgrimages, and he seems to have imagined that he would not recover, for he wrote the Governor-General the farewell letter which follows. It is chiefly interesting for the fact that it mentions his giving over his estates to his eldest son, Lal Chutter Sahee, and yet at the time of his death he left, as we shall see, no children of his own. We must, therefore, presume that Lal Chutter Sahee predeceased him, which led to his making use of the right of adoption shortly before his death, in 1832. His letter addressed to Lord Amherst read:

From Rajah Oodwunt Sinha. Received December 6, 1822.

After Compliments.

Your Lordship must have been informed by the letters of the officer commanding the battalion of Hazaree Bagh of my fidelity, obedience, and attachment to the Company, and I have taken the liberty of addressing you on my own affairs, as I consider myself solely under your protection. In the month of September I set out on a pilgrimage to Gaiyagu, where I arrived in good health, and I greatly relieved myself by the performance of the object of my journey. On the approach of the Doorgah Poojah, I paid a visit to Maharajah Sirdat Nath Singh, Zemindar of the pergunnah of Ramgurh, at Eechak, in the Zillah of Ramgurh. I had intended a few days, after I had paid a visit to the officer of Hazaree Bagh, to have returned home. I unluckily have fallen so ill at this place that I have no hopes of recovery, and, inasmuch as this life is transitory and perishable, what cause of astonishment is there if the thread of my existence be cut short? This being the case, I hope that Your Lordship will look with kindness upon my eldest son, Lal Chutter Sahee (who has arrived at the age of manhood, and is very clever, and into whose charge, previous to my departure, I gave all the business of my zemindaree and of my house), so that he may be prosperous under the effect of your favour, and, having confirmed him in the possession of the lands of the zemindaree, he will always be employed in praying for your prosperity.

Udwant Sinha lived nearly ten years after this letter, and his male descendants having died out, he adopted, as he had full right to do, his nephew, Ram Chand, the son of his youngest brother, Janki Ram Sinha. There appears to have been some doubt as to the adoption having been fully completed at the time of his death, but the point is not very material to our narrative, which is chiefly concerned with showing how the family title came back into the elder line.

Udwant Sinha was undoubtedly a clever man, but he had got his title surreptitiously and by concealing the fact that his elder brother had left an heir. The Government had recognized him as Rajah simply and solely because he was believed to be, and accepted as, the head of his family. During his life he was probably too powerful and too much feared for anyone to let out the facts, but after he was dead there was no longer any restraint, and the intention of his adopted son, Ram Chand, to claim the headship of the family brought the rightful heir to the front. Kumar Kissan Chand, the eldest son of Hanumanta, the eldest son of Bahadur Sinha, appeared on the scene. The story is told in the following letter:

To G. Swinton, Esq., Chief Secretary to Government, Fort William.

SIR,

I have the honour to forward two arzees from Kumar Kishen Chund—one to the address of the Right Honourable the Governor-General, the other the Honourable the Vice-President. The object of the Kumar is to obtain from Government the confirmation of the title of Rajah Bahadur, which has been for several generations in the family of which he considers himself the representative. It will be seen by the accompanying sketch that he is the son of the eldest son of Rajah Bahadur Sinha, who died in 1811.

2. On the death of Rajah Bahadur Sinha, the right of his eldest son, Hanumanta Sinha, to succeed would seem undoubted. He survived his father from nine to eleven months. No application appears to have been made by him to Government to obtain his investiture, nor is it, I believe, usual to do so during the period of mourning; but on his death Mr. Brooke forwarded to Government a letter from Baboo Oodwunt Sinha, the brother of Hanumanta Sinha, reporting the death of their father, Rajah Bahadur Sinha, and soliciting for himself the title, passing over without notice the claim, and even the existence, of his infant nephew, the present applicant. Government was pleased, on August 14, 1812, to recognize Oodwunt Sinha's right to assume the title, stating expressly, however, that his right was recognized on the supposition that he was the eldest son of his father and the representative of the family. I must conclude the Superintendent of Nizamut affairs was ignorant of the existence of a child whose rights would appear incontestable, for on October 31 he reported to Government his having conferred on Oodwunt Sinha the Khellat of investiture, stating distinctly that he was the representative of the family.

3. Previous to his death, Rajah Oodwunt Sinha had determined to adopt Ram Chand, the son of his youngest brother, deceased. It is denied by the present applicant that the adoption was completed; but he urges that, if it were, Oodwunt Sinha could not transmit to an adopted child a title the recognition of which he had himself obtained only by a fraudulent concealment.

I have, etc.,

MURSHIDABAD, T. H. A. COBBE.

January 2, 1832.

RAJAH KRISHNA CHUNDER SINHA BAHADUR.

To face page 98.

TRANSLATION OF AN ARZEE FROM KUMAR KISHEN CHUND TO THE GOVERNOR-GENERAL.

Received January 4, 1832.

Rajah Devi Sinha, elder brother of my grandfather, Rajah Bahadur Sinha, having come from the Upper Provinces to reside in the city of Moorshedabad, was invested by the British Government with an honorary robe and the title of Rajah Bahadoor. He was succeeded by my grandfather, Rajah Bahadur Sinha, to whom the favour and kindness of the British Government was similarly extended. Rajah Bahadur Sinha died leaving three sons, Hanimant Sinha, my father, being the eldest, and Oodwunt Sinha and Jankuram Sinha, my uncles, the second and third. My father died a few months after him, leaving me a mere infant.

On account of his being at that time the senior, my uncle, Rajah Oodwunt Sinha, received the robe and title of Rajah Bahadur, according to the custom of the family, and to the end of his life he was honoured with the friendship and good wishes of the British authorities. He is now dead, leaving me and my three younger brothers his heirs.

According to the usage of the family, the headship of the house and the control of all their domestic concerns, the hereditary zemindary, etc., rest and remain in me, the representative and chief. I therefore trust to Your Lordship's kindness that, in conformity with the custom observed towards my ancestors, I may be honoured by Your Lordship with the robe and title, by which means I shall be accredited and exalted in the eyes of my peers and kinsfolk.

Kissan Chand was, of course, duly recognized, but the Government, rendered a little cautious by the fact that it had been imposed upon, took several precautions, and, among other persons, wrote to Ram Chand to inquire what he had to say about it. His reply was as follows:

Your very kind letter, dated April 16 of the present year, mentioning that my eldest brother, Babu Kishen Chund, had presented an arzee to be submitted to the Right Honourable the Governor-General, stating that he is the eldest son of Hanumant Sinha, and that Hanumant Sinha was the eldest son of Rajah Bahadur Sinha, and that Rajah Bahadur was the brother of the late Rajah Devi Sinha Bahadur, with the hope of obtaining the title of Rajah in consequence of his being the representative of the family, and for me to state whether this statement was correct, and to mention the grounds of objection, should I have any, has been duly received, and with the tenor of which I have been duly informed.

To the application made by my eldest brother I have not the slightest objection, nor is the statement furnished by him in any degree objectionable; however, as my late father, Oodwunt Singh Bahadur, held a title, I think myself entitled to the same indulgence from the British Government.

Although Ram Chand in this letter feigned to be satisfied, he was really nothing of the kind, and resorted to all kinds of low intrigues to get the better of his cousin and to appropriate as much of the property that rightfully belonged to the head of the family as he could possibly secure. The opinion held in Nashipur itself was that Ram Chand was an intriguing and most unprincipled man who would stop at nothing to secure his ends. His one idea was to receive for himself the succession to the Raj, and with this object in view he instituted several civil and even criminal actions against his cousin, Kumar Kissan Chand, both at Murshidabad and Calcutta. The seal of the State and valuable jewellery belonging to the Raj were retained and concealed by him.

He even resorted to fabricating false deeds, upon which he based action in the Courts, and on some of these decrees favourable to himself were made. Not content with these measures, he carried off and concealed for a long time Kumar Udoy Chand, Kissan Chand's younger son, but the climax of his conduct was to institute a criminal action against his cousin in the Calcutta High Court. In the end, all his charges were refuted and his schemes collapsed. Under all the circumstances, Kissan Chand behaved with great generosity in agreeing to a compromise, by which Ram Chand was assigned one pargannah for his support in settlement of all his claims. The Government ignored his application for permission to use the title of Rajah.

The following is the official letter signed by Sir Charles Metcalfe, recognizing Kissan Chand as Rajah Bahadur:

Your arjee (application), containing many thanks and praises for your having obtained the titles of Rajah and Bahadur, and praying for a sunnud and khelat concerning the same, and containing also manifestations of loyalty to the Sovereign and other matters, has reached me and laid before my eyesight, and the matters therein contained made known. The thanks and praises which have been expressed, having manifested abundant loyalty and well-wishes to the Sovereign, it has given me greatest satisfaction.

Whereas your ancestors were specially connected and related with this Raj Sircar, which is the abode of highest dignity, a set of Khelat dress is sent for you through Major Cobbe. It is proper that you should consider the same as your greatest benefit, that you shall thereby adorn your body, which is filled with loyalty to the Sovereign, and shall for ever be engaged in wishing well to this Raj Sircar, which is the abode of the highest dignity. And whereas it is not necessary for a *separate and new sunnud for the title*, this letter will be *abundantly efficacious for the sunnud of this title*. What more is to be written?

C. T. METCALFE.

December 8, 1832.

Rajah Kissan Chand was so much occupied with the litigation arising from his cousin's proceedings that he had little time to attend to other matters. He was suddenly carried off by cholera in the year 1850, leaving his immense estate to his eldest son, Kirti Chand Sinha. At this time, the Nashipur Raj was a vast territory administered directly by its Rajahs and with all the makings of an independent state in it. The jaghirs, zemindaries, and pargannahs acquired by Devi Sinha and his brother, and added to by Udwant Sinha, passed practically without diminution into the possession of Kirti Chand Sinha.

At the time of his father's death Kirti Chand was a minor, and it was only on November 16, 1852, on reaching his eighteenth birthday, that he was recognized formally as Rajah Bahadur at a special Durbar held for the purpose by the Governor-General's agent at Murshidabad. But Kirti Chand was given to pleasure, and, departing from the traditions of his family, neglected his business and allowed himself to be swayed by evil counsellors who thought only of their own interests. In a foolish moment he consented to the sub-letting on permanent leases of his numerous zemindaries in Murshidabad, Birbhum, Rajshahi, Malda, Pubna, and Bogra. This step was taken in what is known in Bengal as the Patni fashion, under the provisions of Regulation VIII. of 1819, but unfortunately for the Nashipur Raj the rents were fixed at a far lower sum than they ought to have been. Neither was any adequate premium paid at the time of taking the leases. Among the tenants of Nashipur were the Nawab Nazim of Bengal, Behar, and Orissa, and several of the most distinguished zemindars of Bengal, and their present representatives still pay their rents for these leased lands into the Nashipur treasury.

Having been the first of his house to diminish its importance, Rajah Kirti Chand died in 1864, at the early age of thirty. After his death, and during the minority of Ranajit Sinha, the management of the family estates and affairs was taken over to their great advantage by the Court of Wards.

CHAPTER VI

DESCRIPTION OF THE NASHIPUR RAJ

IN order to exactly appreciate the position of Nashipur, it is necessary to begin by saying something about Murshidabad, the district in which it is placed. Murshidabad, the former capital of Bengal, was, at the time that Devi Sinha established himself in that province, one of the finest and most prosperous cities in India. Its bankers of the famous Seth family were the financial magnates of the East. Its streets were lined with palaces, and all the Englishmen who visited it in the eighteenth century descanted on its splendour. In 1759 Clive described it as being as extensive, populous, and rich as London, with individuals possessing infinitely greater property than those in the English metropolis. It is situated on the Bhagirathi, one of the seven channels of the Ganges, and a river sacred among the Hindus. The following is the legendary story of the river:

"Raja Sagar of Ajodhya, who lived in pre-historic days, desirous of performing the great sacrifice of the horse, had entrusted a beautiful animal with his son Asamanja, which, however, was stolen by Indra. Sagar ordered his 60,000 sons to search and find out the horse. In their errands they entered subterraneous regions where the fire of the wrath of Basendeva, disguised as Kapila, reduced them to ashes. For their salvation Suparna, a maternal relative of the family, suggested oblations with the water of the

Ganges, which was then in Heaven. Bhagirath, the great-great-grandson of Sagar, after one thousand and one years of austere supplication, succeeded in propitiating Brahma and bringing down the Ganges, which flowed in seven streams, one of which followed the car of Bhagirath, who, bent upon effecting the salvation of his great-grand-uncles, proceeded sounding his gong-shell to the regions underneath where they had perished. This stream thence became known as the Bhagirathi, possessing great sanctity, and credited for centuries without number as the great purifier of sins and the saviour of the fallen.

"Apart from this prehistoric origin, the Bhagirathi is said to represent the old channel of the Ganges, which latterly took an easterly course and formed what is now known as the Pudma, a change which cut off the principal cities in Lower Bengal, reducing the river, which was the great trade route through which the treasures of the country found their way to European marts, to a petty stream barred here and there by sand-banks. In fact, the whole course of the River Ganges and the Bhagirathi from the Himalayan Mountains to the sea (Gangasagar) is regarded by the Hindus as the sacred river *Ganga*. Most of the principal towns in Northern India are situated on its banks, such as Hardwar, Allahabad, Mirzapur, Benares, Patna, Monghyr, Bhagulpur, Murshidabad, Berhampur, Cutwa, Culna, Santipur, Hugli, and Calcutta. It is said that Surajud-Dowla, apprehensive that the English would in their ships-of-war pass up and down the river, caused immense piles to be driven into its bed, which facilitated the silting up of the river."

Murshidabad is consequently situated in the centre of holy territory in the eyes of the Hindus, but it owes its origin to the Mahomedans, for there seems no doubt that it was founded in the reign of Akbar. We have seen how Tarawan, the earliest known ancestor of the Maharajah of Nashipur, was drawn from Bejapur to Umballa by the attraction of its holiness as a place of pilgrimage, and when Devi Sinha quitted Delhi for the Gangetic Delta, it was probably religious fervour that made him select the banks of the Bhagirathi as the site of his new home.

Nashipur is situated on the left bank of the Baghirathi, about a mile north of the city. The Raj covers an area of about 340,000 acres, and is computed to produce a revenue of about £100,000 a year. It is one of the most fertile tracts of Bengal, and the Raj has been admirably managed for a period of 150 years.

The Rajbari, or residence of the Maharajah, is a palatial building, and it is recorded that when Lord Curzon visited it he declared that "it was a splendid mansion, better than ours."

The following description is taken from the "Musnud of Murshidabad": "The Raj premises occupy a large area, and comprise the Thacoorbati, in the principal temple of which is located the family deity, Sri Sri Ram Chandra Deb Thacoor. In the inner quadrangle of the Thacoorbati a niche or room is allotted to each one of the countless images that receive their daily worship. The Sheba is well managed by the present Shebait, Maharaja Ranajit Sinha, who performs the several annual festivities in connection with the Sheba, especially the Jhoolun, with great splendour. Vast zemindaries have been dedicated for the worship of the Thacoors. The fact of this endowment was communicated to the Governor-General by a letter received in Calcutta on December 6, 1819, and his consent was conveyed through the agent at Murshidabad.

"The main building of the Rajbati, which is a two-storeyed house with a grand flight of stairs, has an imposing façade. The large and spacious drawing-room is well furnished and upholstered. Two valuable paintings, the portraits of Rajah Keertichand Bahadar and Kumar Udoy Chandra, adorn the walls. The Viceroy, Lord Curzon, who paid a visit to the Rajbati, is reported to have said,

'I do not agree with you when you say yours is a humble house; it is better than ours. It is a princely abode.'

"The principal palace was constructed by Rajah Kurtichand Bahadur. The founder of the family—namely, Debi Singh of history—settled at Bokhara, where his Thacoorbati still exists. Rajah Bahadur Singh removed and settled at Gaisabad, and thence removed to Nashipore. The Raj residence is situated by the side of the Grand Trunk road leading from Calcutta to the United Provinces.

"The upper flat of the western block contains the drawing-room, Durbar Hall, dining-room, dressing-rooms, the Maharajah's office, his study, etc. The lower flat contains the Raj public office, the offices of the Dewan and Naib Dewan, the Treasury, the Library, the Record department, and other offices. The northern and eastern blocks are reserved for the ladies."

Nashipur is very easily accessible, for it has a railway station of its own on the Murshidabad branch-line of the Eastern Bengal State Railway, and all trains up and down stop there. There is another station at Azimganj, only two miles distant. This is on a branch line of the East Indian Railway. Azimganj is on the western side of the Bhagirathi, but boats are always available for the passage, and carriages in waiting at the landing-stage. There is also communication by water, as during the wet season, from July to October, the Calcutta Steam Navigation Company run a steamer on the Bhagirathi from Azimganj to Berhampur. Metalled roads have been laid down by the Maharajah's care to the steamer ghât and also to the railway stations. It is scarcely necessary to add that there is a post-office at Nashipur, which does a large postal and telegraphic business.

It is not surprising, considering its position in the northern part of the Gangetic delta, to find that Nashipur is both exceedingly hot and exceedingly damp. During a few months of the winter the climate is more endurable,

THE MAHARAJAH AND HIS FAMILY.

To face page 106.

but it is always more or less trying. On the other hand, the great heat acting on the humid soil explains the extraordinary productiveness of the crops. The most prevalent and fatal of all the diseases from which the people suffer is malaria. The population of the Raj is about 150,000 souls.

I am indebted to Dewan Surada Prosad Mukherji for the following very full particulars of the natural productions of Nashipur, the occupations of its people, their caste divisions, and the scale of payment for the different trades and industries:

Rice is the staple crop within the Raj. This crop is principally of two kinds—*aus* and *aman*.

The *aus*, which is also called *bhadni*, is the coarser kind of rice, consumed by the low-class people. It is sown in April, and reaped in September.

The *aman* is the finer quality of rice, consumed by the well-to-do classes. It is sown in August, and reaped in December.

Khai, *muri*, and *chira* are different preparations of rice, generally used by the people at large for purposes of light refreshments. These become very palatable when mixed with *ghee* (clarified butter), sweets, and spices.

Other principal crops are wheat (*gam*) and barley (*tab*). These are sown in October, and harvested in April.

Various sorts of pulses (*dal*) are cultivated, such as: (1) *Mug*, of which there are three varieties—(*a*) *sona mug*, (*b*) *ghora mug*, (*c*) *krishna mug*; sown in September, and reaped in December. (2) *Kalai*, of two varieties—*kali kalai* and *mosh kalai*; sown in September, and reaped in December. (3) *Arhar*, which includes *tungur*; sown in April, and reaped in March. (4) *Bút* (*grum*), (5) *matar*, (6) *musuri*, (7) *khesari*; these are sown in October, and reaped in February.

Some very coarse grains, such as *kodo*, *syamè*, *bhuta*, and *jai* (oats), are also cultivated.

There are three different sorts of oil seeds: (1) mustard (*sarisa*), sown in October, and reaped in January; (2) linseed (*mosina*), sown in October, and reaped in February; (3) *sesaman* (*til*), sown in October, and reaped in December.

Two varieties of fibres are grown: (1) Jute (*pat* or *koshta*); (2) flax (*son*). These are sown in April, and reaped in September.

The mulberry (*tutpat*) cultivation is carried on on an extensive scale. It is a perennial plant, and very profitable.

The sugar-cane (*ikshu* or *auk*) is sown in March, and gathered in January.

The indigo cultivation was at one time very considerable, but has been almost given up since the introduction of the artificial dye.

The betel-leaf (*pan*) is also a perennial plant, and most profitable.

The tobacco is sown in December, and reaped in March.

The potato is sown in September, and reaped in March.

The onion is sown in October, and reaped in April.

Fruits.

1. Mangoe (*amra*), plucked in May and June.
2. Jack (*kanthal*), plucked in June and July.
3. Cocoanut (*narikal*), plucked in September and October.
4. Plantain (*rambha* or *kala*), perennial.
5. *Bel* or *sriphal*, plucked in February and March.
6. Apple (*ata*), plucked in October.
7. *Papeya*, perennial.
8. *Goava* (*peara*), plucked in December.
9. Plum (*kul*), plucked in January.

Table showing the quantity produced, or out-turn of crop, in a bigha of land (the ordinary bigha in Bengal contains 1,600 sqrare yards):

Crop	Yield	Crop	Yield
1. Rice (*aus*)	8 maunds	10. *Khesaree*	5 maunds
„ (*aman*)	10 „	11. Mustard (*sarisa*)	3 „
2. Wheat (*gam*)	5 „	12. Linseed (*mosina*)	2 „
3. Barley (*jab*)	4 „	13. Sesaman (*til*)	2 „
4. Mug (*sona*)	2 „	14. Oats (*jai*)	4 „
„ (*ghora* or *krishna*)	3 „	15. Jute (*pat*)	4 „
5. *Kalai*	5 „	16. Flax (*son*)	2 „
6. *Arhar*	5 „	17. Potatoes	10 „
7. Gram (*bút*)	6 „	18. Tobacco	2 „
8. Peas (*matar*)	5 „	19. Sugarcane	10 „
9. *Musuri*	3 „	20. Onion	20 „

(A bazaar maund=72·33 lbs.)

Table showing the price of foodstuffs:

Good rice (*atab*)	Rupees 6 per maund
„ (*usna*)	„ 5 „
Common rice	„ 4.8 „
Wheat	„ 3.4 „
Barley	„ 2 „
Mug (*sona*)	„ 6.4 „
„ (*ghora* or *krishna*)	„ 4.4 „
Kalai (*kali*) / „ (*mash*)	„ 3.12 „
Arhar	„ 2.10 „
Gram	„ 2.4 „
Peas (*matar*)	„ 2.4 „
Musuree	„ 2.8 „
Khesaree	„ 1.10 „

Vegetables.

1. *Bagan*, sown in July, and gathered from October.
2. *Patal*, sown in September, and gathered from March.
3. *Alu*, three varieties:

   Golalu, sown in October, and reaped in February.

   Sankerkund, sown in September, and reaped in April.

   Sankalu, sown in July, and reaped in January.

4. *Mala* (radishes), sown in October, and reaped in December.
5. *Jhinga*, sown in April, and reaped in July.

6. *Karla*, sown in May, and reaped in October.

7. *Rampatal*, sown in July, and reaped in September.

8. *Kachu* (*makhi*), sown in May, and reaped in September.

9. *Kumra* (*surya*), sown in June, and reaped in September.

10. *Lasa*, sown in June, and reaped in September.

11. *Khero*, sown in February, and reaped in April.

Industries.

1. There are many silk filatures (*banaks*) within the Raj, and a great number of people are employed there. These filatures are found in places where the mulberry plant thrives well. The mulberry plantation is very profitable, and cocoons are reared in many places where these plants are easily available.

The winding of silk is the principal manufacture within the Raj. The weaving of silk cloths—*kora* or *garod*, *matka*, and *tussar* of various sorts and designs—also forms another branch of the industry of considerable importance. But this silk industry is not now in a flourishing state.

2. The indigo industry has now considerably fallen off, and many factories within the Raj have been closed. All that tract of land lying by the side of the Ganges, the Padma, and the Bhagirathi, called *chur* or *diarah*, was at one time utilized solely for the cultivation of indigo; but since the introduction of the artificial dye this industry has almost been given up, and the distinguished firms of Messrs. Jardine, Skinner, and Co., and Messrs. Robert Watson and Co., big leaseholders under the Raj, paying an annual rental of about 50,000 rupees, have withdrawn from it. Their successors have since registered their names, and are carrying on zemindary and other business under the name and style of the Mednipur Zemindary Company, Ltd.

3. The greater portion of the Azimganj Branch Line of the East Indian Railway passes over land comprised in

the Raj. The East Indian Railway Loop Line also runs through a portion of the Raj territories, measuring about forty miles in length.

The newly-constructed Murshidabad Branch Line of the Eastern Bengal State Railway also passes through a portion of this estate.

4. Several machines are at work within the Raj intended for breaking stones for the supply of ballast, etc., to railway companies and municipal corporations, the proprietors whereof are Indian gentlemen.

CASTES.

The higher castes in order of precedence:

1. *Brahmin* (spiritual guide and preceptor).
2. *Kshetriya* (warrior caste).
3. *Vaisya* (trading caste).

After them come—

4. *Vaidya* (physicians).
5. *Kayasta* (writer caste).

The Intermediate Castes.

6. *Napit* (barber).
7. *Kamar* (blacksmith).
8. *Kumar* or *Kumbhakar* (potter).
9. *Goala* (keepers of cows).
10. *Sadgop* (cultivating class).
11. *Vaisnav* (mendicants).
12. *Teli* (trader).
13. *Tamli* (pan-seller).
14. *Gundhabanick* (shopkeeper).
15. *Barni* (pan-seller).
16. *Modak*, *Moira*, or *Halowai* (sweetmeat sellers).
17. *Aguri* or *Ugrakshetri* (cultivator).

The Inferior Castes.

17. *Kansaris* (braziers).
18. *Shankaris* (dealers in *Sauko*).
19. *Kaibarta* (there are two classes—one class cultivate land, the other sell fish).
20. *Chasadhopa* (cultivator).
21. *Tanti* (weavers).
22. *Sarnakar* (goldsmiths).
23. *Subarnabanick* (merchants).
24. *Jugee* (weavers).
25. *Chhutar* (carpenters).
26. *Suri* (spirit sellers).
27. *Kalu* (oil seller).
28. *Dhoba* (washerman).
29. *Chunari* (lime burners).
30. *Dulya*
31. *Kahar*
32. *Behara*
33. *Bagdee*

} (palanquin bearers and labourers).

34. *Pura* or *Pundarikakshya* (rearers of cocoons, traders, and labourers).
35. *Chain* (cultivators).
36. *Jalia, malo* (fishermen).
37. *Rajbunshe* (cultivators).

Low Castes.

38. *Bhuimelee* (cultivators).
39. *Teor* (cultivators and fishermen).
40. *Mal* (labourers).
41. *Buna* (labourers).
42. *Lat* (domestic servants and labourers).
43. *Dosadh* (labourers).
44. *Dom* (street sweepers and carriers of dead bodies).
45. *Bedeya* (jugglers).
46. *Chamar* (shoemakers).

47. *Muchee* (shoemakers).
48. *Hari* (swineherds and sweepers).
49. *Mehtor* (sweepers).

The population is composed of Hindus, Mahomedans, and Santhals.

Except the landholding class, the merchant traders, and professional men, the bulk of the people are engaged in agricultural pursuits and daily labour; some are in Government employ and private service.

Table showing average daily wages of labourers (the anna = a penny, and there are sixteen annas to the rupee):

1.	Goldsmiths (*sarnokar*)	10 annas to 1 rupee.
2.	Blacksmiths (*karmokar*)	8 to 12 annas.
3.	Carpenters (*chhutar*)	8 to 12 annas.
4.	Masons (*rajmistrus*)	8 to 10 annas.
5.	Painters (*chitrakar*)	8 to 12 annas.
6.	Chupperbund (*gharam[illegible]e*)	7 annas.
7.	Silk spinners	4 to 8 annas.
8.	Malees	5 to 8 annas.
9.	Day labourers	5 to 7 annas.
10.	Palkee bearers	8 annas.

CHAPTER VII

RANAJIT SINHA

RANAJIT SINHA, the present Maharajah, was born on June 9, 1865. As already stated, his estates were placed during his minority under proper management, and he was himself made a ward of the Court. When he reached a suitable age he was sent to the Berhampur College, which is close to Murshidabad and Nashipur. Here he made good progress at his lessons and was especially distinguished in mathematics. He gained the approbation of his masters more particularly by his diligence and regularity in attendance; and they predicted for him an honourable and successful career when he should succeed to his inheritance. Nor has the prediction been falsified by the result.

When he approached his eighteenth birthday (the coming-of-age date in India), he married, on May 4, 1883, Kamal Kumari, the eldest daughter of Bahu Giridhari Lall, of Calcutta, and the marriage has proved singularly happy. It has been blessed with a large family, of whom there will be more to be said hereafter. In 1886, on reaching the age of twenty-one, Ranajit Sinha was entrusted with the management of his estates, and at once devoted himself to the task with strenuous energy. He drew up his own "rules for the management of the Nashipur Raj Estate," and these are so simple and excellent that they have been taken as a model by many others of the great landowners

THE DARBAR HALL.

To face page 114.

of Bengal. Under these rules the officers of the Raj enjoy regular privileges, such as leave, pension, sick allowances, and promotion, which were things unknown and undreamt of in the days of Devi Sinha. The young nobleman not only drew up a code of regulations, but he has taken good care ever since that they shall be faithfully observed and carried out.

The first few years of Maharajah Ranajit Sinha's rule were somewhat clouded by a lawsuit with his aunt, who claimed more than her share out of the estate. The Maharajah took personal charge of the case, instructing the lawyers and drafting their briefs himself, and in the end he won the day. By the system of administration he has adopted, it is hoped that all possibility of fruitless and expensive litigation in the future has been avoided.

Immediately after taking over personal control of his Raj, the Maharajah began what may be called his public career. In 1887 he was appointed an honorary magistrate of the Lalbag Independent Bench, and in the following year he was elected Chairman of the Murshidabad Municipality. During his term of office he introduced many sanitary and other reforms, which earned him the gratitude of the whole community.

His popularity was immensely enhanced by his conduct during the celebrated floods of 1888, when the Bhagirathi overflowed its banks and carried destruction far and wide in the Murshidabad district. He took an active part, not merely in saving many people from drowning, but also in providing for a large number of starving families, whose means of sustenance had been destroyed. His conduct on this occasion was highly appreciated by Sir Stuart Bayley, then Lieutenant-Governor of Bengal. It was shortly after these incidents that the young Prince was recognized by the Government as Rajah, and the late Sir Charles Elliott went to Murshidabad in person to preside over the durbar of investiture and recognition. The ceremony took place on March 4, 1892, and the following is an extract from the Governor's speech on the occasion:

> It is a very great pleasure to me to convey to you the sanad of the title of Rajah which the Viceroy has been pleased to confer upon you. The title is one which had *been honourably borne by your family for many generations*, and it is now committed to you to hold untarnished. One of your ancestors, Rajah Devi Sinha, *rendered very valuable services to Clive at Plassey, and the continued favour in which your family has been held, and the honour which is to-day entrusted to you* is a proof that the Government of India is never slow to recognize and never forgets services rendered to it by the ruling houses in this country. You have lately attained your majority and succeeded to your property. I trust you will manage your estate in a manner worthy of your ancestry, and that your career may compare favourably with that of other zemindars in the province; and that it will be so distinguished that further honours will be conferred upon you, not on account of the good work of those who have gone before you, but as a reward of your own merit and exertions.

It will be noticed that the title conferred on this occasion was that of Rajah alone, but it was soon supplemented by the coveted addition of Bahadur, to which Ranajit Sinha had a prescriptive family right. This second presentation was made in January, 1897, by Sir Charles Stevens, who spoke as follows:

> Rajah, you are a scion of a very ancient and respectable family and the proprietor of extensive zemindaries, and you have conducted yourself in a manner worthy of your origin and of your rank and responsibilities. You have the reputation of being a good and liberal landlord to your own ryots, but your desire to do good service to the public has led you to enter a more extended sphere of usefulness. As a municipal commissioner and an honorary magistrate, you have rendered great assistance to the local authorities. It has been deemed just and proper that you should be raised to the dignity which your father enjoyed. You have therefore been created a Rajah Bahadur, and it gives me great satisfaction to hand you the sanad and the khillat which mark your elevation to that rank.

His first notable public act was in the year 1887, when he celebrated the Jubilee of the Queen-Empress Victoria the Good, by the construction of a splendid public hall, in the heart of the city of Murshidabad, which is still known as "Kumar Ranajit Sinha's Jubilee Hall." At the time he had not received his title of Rajah, and was consequently only a Kumar, or an expectant. This hall is an ornament to the city, and contains, in addition to the main saloon, many minor rooms, which are used as reading rooms and for committee meetings. The hall is used for all public meetings, and also for entertainments and festivities.

Allusion has been made to the fact that in 1888 he was elected to the office of Chairman of the Murshidabad Municipality. He was re-elected in 1889, and again for the last time in 1903, and held the post altogether for a period of ten years. During this term, he devoted a great part of his attention to the improvement of the sanitary condition of the city. His main objects were the supply of pure drinking-water and the provision of free dispensaries and medical aid for the poor. These steps were taken prior to the reform movement in these matters, which has since become so general in India.

One of the most notable works in this direction has been the establishment of a dispensary in his own town of Nashipur. This is called and known as "The Nashipur Raj Dispensary." Medical aid and advice, as well as the best medicines from England, are given here free during the morning and evening hours to all who present themselves. It is placed in charge of a qualified resident medical officer, who is a graduate of the Calcutta Medical College, and he has the assistance of a qualified compounder and dresser. The dispensary is periodically inspected by the Civil surgeon of the district, and the annual returns of its work show that it is doing an immense amount of good to the people of Nashipur and the surrounding places, for its benefits are not restricted to the Maharajah's own dependents and ryots.

In addition to his municipal work the Maharajah took

great interest in his judicial duties. We referred to his being appointed an Honorary Magistrate of the Lalbag Independent Bench soon after attaining his majority. In 1894 he was vested with the powers of a magistrate of the second class, and empowered to sit and try cases alone. In this capacity he displayed so much zeal and ability that the Government, in appreciation of his service, vested him with the powers of a magistrate of the first class on March 1, 1897, and with powers to take cognizance of offences on complaint and police reports. It was during this time that he was placed in entire charge of the Lalbag Bench, and virtually discharged the duties of a sub-divisional officer after the abolition of the Lalbag Division.

It was due to the excellence of his judicial work, and also to the reputation he gained for thoroughness and punctuality in the discharge of his public duties that the Government of India appointed him a member of the Bengal Legislative Council in 1899. We shall deal with his public work in connection with the legislature of the country in the following chapter; but, before passing on to fresh matters, it may be mentioned that he has discharged other public duties than those we have referred to. He was for several years Vice-President of the "British Indian Association," the most ancient land-holders' association in India, and also President of the Murshidabad Association.

The Maharajah is fully alive to the need for, and the benefits of, modern education. He has founded schools in Nashipur for both girls and boys, to which those born on his country estate have also free access. A competent staff of teachers with suitable qualifications in schools and colleges has been appointed. Instruction is given in the Bengal vernacular, but in the upper schools it is combined with English. The Maharajah has founded many scholarships, generally in connection with the official visits paid on the occasion of his investiture with higher rank and honours. One of these was in honour of Sir Edward Norman Baker, the last Lieutenant-Governor of Bengal, and was tenable for two years by the student standing first at the intermediate Arts examination of the Calcutta University. Another benefaction of this character was the annual presentation of a gold medal in honour of the late Sir Alexander Mackenzie, at one time Lieutenant-Governor of Bengal, to be awarded to the student standing first in mathematics in the Matriculation examination at the same University.

Perhaps the most remarkable feature in the Maharajah's character is that, despite the enervating nature of the Bengal climate, he is, and has always been, most assiduous in his attention to business. He attends his office regularly from eleven to five; and during the cold weather he makes a tour through the mofussil, visiting all his estates in turn, and going closely into details of management, and discussing modern improvements with his tenants. It is therefore said of him that he can at any moment enter into the details of his zemindary works with a precision and knowledge of detail that excite admiration.

Considering his good work, and the example he sets to the other great landowners of Bengal, it is not remarkable that the Government decided to increase his honour. It remembered that his ancestor, Rajah Devi Sinha, had borne the title of Maharajah, and it decided to revive the style in favour of Ranajit Sinha. Sir Edward Norman Baker was entrusted with the pleasant mission of making the investiture, including the bestowal of a suitable khillat, or dress of honour. On this occasion (January 1, 1910) he delivered the following address:

It is always a matter of gratification to me to be the instrument for conveying marks of public recognition to those who have deserved well of the State. That pleasure is much enhanced when the recipient of the honour is an old and valued friend of my own. In your case our *friendship dates back to the year* 1898, *when we both were serving on the Bengal Council, and when I first learnt to appreciate in you those qualities of rectitude, sincerity, straightforwardness, and moderation* which have given you so high a place in my regard.

The family of which you are the head is both old and distinguished, and one member of it enjoyed the title of Maharajah as long ago as the year 1800—more than a century ago. Twice already you yourself have received marks of the favour of Government—in 1892 and again in 1897—and it gives me peculiar pleasure now to hand you the sanad of the still higher title of Maharajah, together with the khillat which accompanies it.

This honourable distinction you have worthily earned, not merely by service in a variety of public offices, as chairman of the Murshidabad municipality, as an honorary magistrate, as member of the Legislative Council, and the like, but still more by the loyal and devoted spirit which you have invariably displayed in times of difficulty and temptation, and by the influence which you have uniformly exerted to counteract the evil forces of sedition, and to further the cause of law, order, and good government. I am hopeful that this influence will be further strengthened by the honourable preferment which you have now received, and which I earnestly hope you will live long to enjoy.

The conference of this higher honour was made the occasion of great popular rejoicing. On the return of His Highness from Calcutta on March 6, 1910, he received a great public ovation which may be summarized from the paper of the day:

. . . The Maharajah of Nashipur and family arrived here yesterday morning. A hearty and enthusiastic reception was accorded to him. The town of Nashipur was decorated with triumphal arches, flags, festoons, and evergreens, and presented a grand and unique spectacle. Universal joy prevailed in the town. In the afternoon, the ladies presented an address of congratulation in a beautiful silver casket to the Maharani. The Maharajah received two addresses, one from Nashipur and another from Iohaganj. In joint reply, he thanked the gentlemen for their congratulations and for the grand reception accorded to him. He expressed gratification that his public services were appreciated by his countrymen. He regretted that his waterworks scheme could not be carried out. He expressed his heartfelt gratitude to His Honour the Lieutenant-Governor for conferring on him this new distinction.

In conclusion, he addressed the assembly in Bengalese at some length on the present situation, and explained in clear and emphatic tones the manifold advantages of British rule and the mischief caused to the country by anarchical and seditious movements. He asked the

MAHARAJ KUMAR BHUPENDRA NARAYAN SINHA.

To face page 120.

people to heartily co-operate with the Government in preventing and detecting crimes. He exhorted schoolboys not to mix in politics, and explained to their tutors and guardians their heavy responsibility in keeping their pupils and wards aloof from all political agitations. In his opinion, nothing should be done to create or encourage racial feeling between the rulers and the ruled. The Europeans and Indians are all subjects of the same mighty sovereign. Amity and goodwill should prevail amongst them.

Three weeks later the formal reception of the Maharajah by the residents of the Murshidabad district was held in the city, and the account of it given by the chief Bengal newspaper is full of interesting details. The meeting was noteworthy for the unanimity displayed by its English, Hindu, and Mahomedan supporters:

MURSHIDABAD,
March, 29.

A grand and most enthusiastic reception was given to the Maharajah of Nashipur by the residents of the district at a splendid pavilion, specially constructed for the purpose, in Murshidabad city, on Monday, March 28, at 6 p.m. The gathering was of a thoroughly representative character. The Honourable the Maharajah of Kasimbazar, and Nawab Nasirul Mamalek Sajatoli Beg expressed regret at their inability to be present. The Maharajah, escorted by a body of mounted volunteers, reached the pavilion precisely in time, and was received at the gate by the Honourable Babu Baikuntha Nath Sen, President of the Reception Committee, and other leading members. The carriage was unhorsed on the way by a body of volunteers, who drew it up to the pandel when people on both sides of the road greeted him with garlands and flowers.

The proceedings commenced with a song specially composed for the occasion. The Honourable President, in an excellent speech, expressed in glowing terms the various public services of the Maharajah as a member of the Bengal Legislative Council, Chairman of the Murshidabad Municipality, first-class Honorary Magistrate, member of the District Board, and President of the Murshidabad Association. He also noticed the great ability shown by the Maharajah in managing his vast estates, and the deep veneration with which he follows the dictates of his religion. He then described the manifold qualities of head and heart which have made the Maharajah so popular. Every right cause, he said, finds in the Maharajah an ardent supporter, and his purse is always open to such cause. As spokesman of the public and as a friend and well-wisher of the Maharajah, he asked him to accept the congratulatory address which the public were going to present, and concluded by praying for a long lease of prosperous life to the Maharajah, and wishing his successors to follow the footsteps of their illustrious father.

The Pandits then chanted benedictory verses, after which Babu Badhinatha Sen, son of the late Dr. Ram Das Sen, and a vakil of the High Court, read and presented the address to the Maharajah. Maulvi Ameer Hossein read the Urdu address. The school girls and boys recited congratulatory verses.

The Maharajah then, in an eloquent speech, thanked the members of the Committee and other gentlemen of the district for the great and unique honour shown to him that evening. He was very grateful to the Government, and specially to Sir Edward Baker, for the new dignity conferred on him, and said that his family yielded to none in the past and would yield to none in the future in its loyalty to the throne and the Government. He observed that during his term of Chairmanship he tried his best to improve the sanitation of the town with the limited resources at the disposal of the Municipality. He noticed with regret that the scheme for the supply of pure drinking water which he nearly brought to completion when his period of office expired is going to be abandoned, but he hoped that his successor would not absolutely give it up, but try to complete it for freeing the town from the epidemics of malaria, cholera, and small-pox. He specially thanked his young friends who attended as volunteers, and willingly observed that, though it is generally believed that title-holders are not liked at all by the rising generation, his case is proved to be an exception. He thought that he did not deserve so much praise for what he had done as a member of the Legislative Council or as an Honorary Magistrate. Whatever he had done he did from a pure sense of duty and from no other consideration, and this, said he, is and would always be the guiding principle of his life.

Babu Janoki Nath Pande then proposed a vote of thanks to the chair, in the course of which he dwelt upon the school career of the Maharajah, of whom he had the honour of being a teacher.

The Maharajah and the gentlemen present were then garlanded by the President and the members. The festivities terminated at about 2 a.m. Never before has Murshidabad witnessed such a grand and hearty reception given to a nobleman by the public at their own cost. Even Europeans came forward with their quota of subscriptions and vied with the native gentlemen in showing honour to the Maharajah.

CHAPTER VIII

RANAJIT SINHA'S PUBLIC WORK.

The public work of Maharajah Ranajit Sinha may be divided into three classes. His participation in the deliberations of the Bengal Legislative Council may be called one; his attention to local needs and questions another; and his utterances on the seditious movements in India the third. Let us take them in their order.

The great question before the Bengal Legislative Council in the year during which the Maharajah held a seat as a member appointed by the Government was the Calcutta Municipal Bill. Some people seemed to think that an "appointed member" was bound to obey the behests of the Government, but the Maharajah—or, rather, the Rajah, as he was at the time—displayed the greatest independence, and thereby earned the respect of the representatives of the Supreme Government. If it is permissible to interpolate a word of general comment, it would be to the effect that the Government of India not merely leaves "appointed members" a free hand, but does not resent criticism and opposition to its measures by such persons if it is made abundantly clear that they are inspired by conscientious motives and a sense of duty. What might be resented would be petty and carping criticism, and wilful obstruction.

The Rajah Ranajit Sinha's conduct was never marked by these traits. When he spoke it was clear that he did so because he felt the need of speaking, and very often he supported the amendments of the official promoters of the Bill, or introduced other amendments which they supported. Although he figured among the opponents of the measure, he accomplished the difficult task of gaining public popularity, and at the same time not alienating the good-will and respectful regard of his official colleagues. Without enlarging too much on this subject, which has now passed to a great extent into the limbo of the forgotten, it will suffice to say that the Rajah made two set speeches on the Bill, which may be left to speak for themselves.

The first of these was delivered on August 7, 1899, and is reported as follows in the official record of the Bengal Legislative Council:

We are grateful to the Government of India for the very kind and sympathetic way in which they have perused various criticisms on the bill, and for the kind assurance they have given that there would be no contravention of the broad principles of local self-government already conceded. The Government is disposed to grant us a concession in the constitution of the General Committee on the model of a standing Committee of Bombay; but, sir, we could not welcome this concession as the number of elected Commissioners in the Corporation is reduced to half, and the Corporation itself is not allowed a free hand in the election of two-thirds of the members of its General Committee like that of Bombay. I think the Government is inclined to reduce the numerical strength of the Corporation in the belief that the existing Corporation has devoted itself to speech and to criticism rather than to action. As I have no personal experience as to the working of the Calcutta municipality I must refrain from making any observation on the point; but the resolutions on the Administrative Reports of the Calcutta Corporation of previous years regarded by your Honour's predecessors in office show that there has been marked and gradual improvement in the administration of the Calcutta Corporation, and that its Commissioners all along have done excellent work. . . .

The present number of Commissioners was fixed after a mature and deliberate consideration, and I do not think that there has been any special necessity to make such a radical change now in that respect. If the Government of India have come to the final determination to reduce the numerical strength of the Corporation, I beg to submit that the reduction should not fall on the shoulders of the elected Commissioners only, as in such a case it will strike at the very root of local self-government, the fundamental principles of which will be violated. If, following the Bombay system, the Government is inclined to reduce the number of elected Commissioners, I beg respectfully to point out that the system proposed to be introduced here materially differs from that adopted in Bombay. The Bombay Corporation elects its own President, and the Standing Committee its own Chairman; but here the official Chairman acts as President of both the Corporation and General Committee; and again in Bombay, though only half the number of Commissioners is elected at ward elections, out of the other half sixteen are elected by Justices, two by Fellows, and only two by the Chamber of Commerce. But here there is no election by Justices or Fellows, and no seat is allowed even to native merchants, or house and landowners; whereas ten seats are allowed to European mercantile communities. So if the Bombay system is at all to be given a trial here I beg to submit that it be adopted in its entirety, and that out of twenty-five seats reserved for nominated and appointed Commissioners, other representative bodies of Calcutta, such as the British Indian Association, the National Chamber of Commerce, the National Mahomedan Association, and the like, should also be allowed to be represented in the Corporation, and the Corporation should be left unfettered in the election of two-thirds of the members of the General Committee. As the Government appoints four members of the General Committee, I humbly think that the Government appointees in the Corporation should have no voice in the election of the rest of the members of the General Committee. In conclusion, I leave the matter in your Honour's hands with the full confidence that under your benign and sympathetic rule our appeal will not go in vain.

The second speech was delivered on September 28, 1899, at the close of the debates and read as follows:

Your Honour, no measure of this Council ever excited so much criticism as the one which we are discussing to-day. I think there is not a single section of the native community left which has not strongly opposed this Bill.

Sir, I am entirely in accord with the principles enunciated by your Honour's predecessor in office, Sir Alexander Mackenzie, from the presidential chair in this Council, prior to and after the introduction of this measure, extracts of which I shall read with your Honour's permission. I do not think that there can be any objection to the hands of the Executive being strengthened for the efficient administration of the Corporation, and that especially in cases of emergency, such as the outbreak of plague, he should have large powers to deal with them, and should not be hampered in any way in the free exercise of his discretion. I also think, sir, that there should be a small executive body interposing between the Chairman and the Corporation to deal with such matters which cannot be properly discussed by the large body, and which are at the same time so important as not to be left to the Chairman alone for disposal; but, sir, I find that the Bill is not limited within the said principle, but has gone far beyond it. Many radical—revolutionary—changes have been introduced. As I have no personal knowledge of the working of the Calcutta Municipality, so I shall only deal with the principles of this Bill. I find larger powers have been given to the Chairman and the General Committee by depriving the Corporation. The Chairman should have been made responsible to somebody, and as the Bill now stands I find he is not, even to Government. In the original Bill the number of the Commissioners was seventy-five, and so heavy powers were given to the General Committee as they could not be properly exercised by such a large body like that; but as it is now reduced to fifty I think further powers should have been given to the Corporation which the Bill reserves for the General Committee. Under the orders of the Government of India, dated June 17 last, the number of the elected Commissioners in the Corporation was reduced on the model of the Bombay system, which will appear from the sixteenth paragraph of the said despatch, in which the Government of India said "they are inclined to think that in a more close adaptation of the Bombay system might be found the solution for which they are seeking." So, sir, I think it would not have been against the principles laid down in the said dispatch if a few seats in the Corporation would have been allowed to other influential representative bodies in Calcutta. I brought forward an amendment to that effect, which was rejected by the Council on the day I could not unfortunately attend, owing to my illness. If that amendment would have been accepted, I am sure it would have pacified to a certain extent the popular feeling, and at the same time would have been in perfect harmony with the Bombay system. As the Corporation is now constituted, the representatives of the ratepayers and the native elements are in a minority, as the number of the elected Commissioners is twenty-five, whereas the number of the appointed Commissioners, including the Chairman, is twenty-six. Then, sir, as to the constitution of the General Committee, which have been vested with all the real powers in Municipal affairs, I find the ratepayers to be in a hopeless minority, and the non-official majority which was in the original Bill has also been practically done away with. I agree that the three chief interests in Calcutta, *i.e.*, ratepayers, men of commerce, and the Government, should be represented in it. In my humble opinion the interests of Government are fully secured even if there would have been no Government nominee in the Committee, as it has kept ample powers of interference and

THE DRAWING-ROOM IN THE RAJBATI.

To face page 126.

supervision in its hand, and, besides that, when its official will always act as President of the Committee. However, the Government certainly required few seats only to rectify the balance and to make up the minorities in the representation. The interests of the ratepayers are great; they constitute the bulk of the population and contribute the bulk of the Municipal rates, and so they should have got a large share of representation in the General Committee. As to the representation of commerce, I find that under the Bill as it now stands four members will be elected, not by the representatives of commerce alone, as was formerly provided, but by the Government appointees. Also the number of the Commissioners appointed by the Government are fifteen, and those nominated by the mercantile communities are ten. If they vote to the full strength of their respective constituent elements the Government appointees will be able to secure those four seats also. So virtually no independent representation of commerce is allowed in the present Bill, which was one of the fundamental principles of this Bill. Sir, I further beg to submit that the present constitution is again based on an illogical solution which the Government of India was so anxious to avoid (*vide* fifteenth paragraph of the despatch) as the representatives of the ratepayers form half the bulk of the Corporation, whereas in the General Committee they bear one-third proportion; and, sir, I am not fully convinced if the Government of India ever contemplated such a change in the constitution of the General Committee as has been done. To my mind it appears rather contrary; I still think that the Government of India contemplated making some concession rather in that respect. If it would have been in their contemplation to bring about such a change they could never have expected that it would be a truce to all dissensions (*vide* last paragraph). Sir, whatever be the case, the Bill as it now stands is certainly worse than what was originally introduced and revised by the Select Committee. As regards the other portions of the Bill, I must admit many improvements have been made though not to our entire expectations. We are thankful to the Select Committee for removing many contentious matters, and especially those relating to cremation of dead bodies and registration of deaths. Sir, I not only consulted many leading landholders who reside in Calcutta and are interested in the matter, but also some of them who have no interest here, and I found all of them opposed to the principles of this Bill; and so, sir, as a representative of the landholders, I think it is my duty to oppose the Bill in its present form. Sir, I shall be wanting in my duty if I fail to acknowledge with gratitude the kindness which you have shown by giving us a patient hearing, and we are at the same time thankful to the honourable member in charge for the courtesy he has all along evinced in the discussion of this measure. With these few remarks I beg most respectfully to oppose the motion.

Apart from the Calcutta Municipal Bill, the Rajah devoted his attention principally to those material questions affecting the sanitary condition of the community and more especially of the inhabitants of the mofussil. The provision of pure drinking water, and the stricter enforcement of the regulation that all local bodies should expend the minimum sum of 5,000 rupees annually on the improvement of the water supply in their districts, were two questions that he several times brought before the Council. He elicited favourable rejoinders from the authorities, and undoubtedly the result of his efforts was that the sanitary authorities in the mofussil were stimulated in their work. He also obtained the concession of increased medical assistance for plague work in the mofussil or country districts. Finally, he secured much-needed protection for Hindu women from assaults by Mahomedan roughs in the Mymensingh district.

The Bengal papers passed the most flattering encomiums on his public work. One paper said: "We did not expect so much zealous work from him"; another congratulated him upon "his public spirit"; and a third declared that he "had done yeoman's work." On the expiration of his term of office, the principal Bengal paper wrote a leading article, from which the following passage is an extract:

"The thanks of the nation are due to the Rajah Ranajit Sinha Bahadur, for not only was he a nominated member, but as a big zemindar residing in the mofussil he risked a good deal by going against the Government in a matter in which the latter showed considerable *zid*. Next to the late ——, no landowner had ever displayed such courage, independence, and patriotism in the Legislative Council as the Rajah Bahadur of Nashipur did. And has he lost in the estimation of the Government? Certainly not. On the other hand, the authorities will now entertain far greater respect for him."

The war in South Africa provided him with the occasion

for displaying his loyalty to the British raj. At the end of January, 1900—that is to say, before the tide of war had fully turned in our favour—he made a strong speech at a public meeting held in the Calcutta Town Hall. The following are the most striking passages from it:

"Your Highness, Maharajahs, Nawabs, Rajahs, and gentlemen,—I feel it an honour and a pleasure to support the resolution just now so ably moved by my worthy and learned friend —— You all know, gentlemen, how the war broke out in South Africa with the Boers, and how the British soldiers are heroically fighting there, and how cheerfully they are laying down their lives for the Sovereign, and for the prestige and glory of the British nation. There can be no shadow of doubt as to the ultimate victory of the British arms. Perhaps you are aware that even men from noble families in England have volunteered their services for the war, and some of them sacrificed their lives in the field. I may mention here the sad but glorious death of the Earl of Ava, and Lieutenant Roberts, one the son of a former Viceroy, and the other the son of the late Commander-in-Chief. In both cases the sympathy of the entire people of India will go forth to the sorrowing parents.

"Gentlemen, this is a time when we, the most loyal subjects of Her Majesty, should come forward to discharge our most sacred duty to our beloved Sovereign. Need I recapitulate the many and various benefits we derive from the British rule. We owe to it our present education, our advancement, and last, but not least, we are indebted to it for the inestimable blessings of peace and prosperity.

"If you advert for a moment to the past, and compare what was then the condition of our country with what it is now, you will, I am sure, again agree with me that we should not have been what we are if Providence had not placed us under the British rule. The benefits of the highest civilization—the highest yet achieved by any nation—have been brought to our doors with very little exertion on our part. Apart from what the British Government is doing for our country we have the sympathy of the British public by our side in time of need. I need not remind you how they helped India at the time of the late famine with their munificent contributions. You may say that the present war does not affect India in any way, but that is surely a very narrow view to take. The more the prestige and the glory of the Government will be upheld, the more will our peace and prosperity be assured. The sooner, therefore, the Government is freed from the anxieties of the war the better it must be for us.

"England is the richest and most powerful country in the world. It may not be necessary for her to take any help from us, but we should still loyally offer any assistance, however insignificant it might be, that lay in our power to give. As citizens of that great Empire, let us, true to the traditions of our country, once more evince our loyalty and attachment to the throne."

A short time after this speech was made, news came of the capture of Pretoria, and the Rajah not only despatched congratulatory telegrams as to his heartfelt joy to the Viceroy, but caused special prayers of thanksgiving to be offered up. The Raj sepoys paraded, the band played the National Anthem, and in the evening the palace and town were illuminated. The sequel of these incidents was that in February, 1902, the Viceroy, Lord Curzon, visited Nashipur and received an ovation in the rajbati, or palace. On this important occasion the Rajah made the following brief address of welcome:

"On behalf of my humble self and the people of Nashipur, I beg to accord to your Excellency a most respectful and loyal welcome, and to assure your Excellency of our staunch loyalty and firm devotion to the throne and person of His Imperial Majesty. I am grateful to your Excellency for the honour you have done me by kindly condescending to stop at my place. I only regret I could not have the honour of welcoming Her Excellency on this occasion. I am desired by my wife to ask you to do her the honour of conveying to Her Excellency her most respectful obeisance. I hope your Excellency's visit to our district will be a pleasant and enjoyable one."

In the course of his reply, Lord Curzon said:

"I thank you for your warm reception. I do not agree with you when you say yours is a humble abode. I see it is a splendid mansion—better than ours. It is a princely abode. I am glad to have the opportunity of witnessing your position and rank. I will convey to Lady Curzon your own and your wife's kind and respectful message. I thank you and the people of Nashipur for your kind reception."

Some years after this visit the disturbed state of Bengal began to attract attention, and more than one outrage startled the public mind. It was then that the Supreme

THE THACKOORBATI AT NASHIPUR.

To face page 130.

Government made an appeal to loyal Indians to come into the open and support its efforts to suppress anarchy and sedition. One of the first to respond was the Maharajah of Nashipur. He made several speeches in support of the British Government, expressing his abhorrence of crime, and calling upon the people of India to testify their loyalty to the British raj by discontinuing seditious talk and upholding the authority of the law. But he felt that something further was required to uphold the title of "loyal Nashipur," so he drew up and circulated the pamphlet which forms the contents of the next chapter.

CHAPTER IX

THE MAHARAJAH'S APPEAL

The following is a literal translation of the Maharajah's appeal in the Bengali language:

"No one is ignorant of the present state of our country. We are frequently hearing of murders, dacoities, and other anarchical crimes. The most regrettable thing is that those who have been proved to be connected with those crimes are almost all Hindus and gentlemen by birth, and the majority of them are not above the age of twenty-one. These imprudent youths have produced baneful results in the country by harbouring in their minds a feeling of hatred against the Government and the British nation, being excited by some irresponsible persons.

"The loyalty and peace-loving disposition of the Indians are well known. The sages who wrote the Hindu Shastras have described murder and treason as heinous sins. Therefore every Hindu is smitten with a sense of shame and grief on seeing his co-religionists concerned in these grievous sins. The introduction of heinous sins in this holy land is a matter to be highly deplored. Whatever is done, if there be sin at its bottom, no good can result therefrom. No country or nation has attained, or can attain, prosperity by having recourse to anarchy and treason. Even in Russia, where assassinations and lawlessness have been prevalent for a long time, such action has led to no good results. Had these hot-headed boys turned their minds towards the welfare of their society and mother-land, without taking to these evil courses, they could probably have done immense good. Pursuing this course of action, these youths could only sacrifice their invaluable lives and take those of some others, but never achieve any good result. What is the good of taking the lives of a few Government officials? The British raj would remain as unaffected as ever, as firm and immovable as the Himalayas. By such acts the interests of the country can only be injured, instead of being advanced.

"Have we no reason to be grateful to the British Government? To whom do we owe our present education and advancement? It is not possible for any other race to maintain peace and order in such a vast country, presenting such diversity of race, language, and religion. To err is human, and it is not impossible that the Government should commit mistakes. But it does not follow that we should impute sinister motives to every Government measure. Its merits and demerits should be considered impartially and with reference to the state of the country. Everyone must frankly admit that peace prevails throughout the land under the British Government; we can go wherever we like without fear of any danger; there is nothing to be feared on the way; there is no apprehension of theft or highway robbery; high education has spread, and is spreading, all over the country; manifold are the advantages we have derived from railways, telegraphs, telephones, etc., in consequence whereof our expenditure has been lessened; the rich do not dare to oppress the poor; everyone is able to follow his own religion without any fear or anxiety, and to spread his religious views unobstructed and unfettered. In any view it must be admitted by everybody, with one voice, that we cannot proceed an inch without the aid of the British Government. Therefore it is our bounden duty to pray wholeheartedly to the All-merciful God that the British

Government may remain for ever unimpaired. Everyone must be up and doing, in order that peace may be restored to the country. It is not at all proper to remain indifferent or apathetic even for a single moment.

"If anyone is of opinion that certain stray individuals may suffer loss or injury on account of the present anarchical state of things—but that the public have no reason to be afraid—then it must be said that his belief is entirely erroneous. If things go on in this way for some time more, it is extremely probable that everyone would be put to trouble and danger. The Government would not be able to devote its time, or find any opportunity to turn its attention, to measures beneficial to us; public money would be unprofitably spent in suppressing lawlessness; the life and property of no man would be safe, and the Government would naturally find reasons to distrust us more and more. It will be forced to enact severe penal laws. In consequence whereof many innocent men will be unnecessarily harassed and humiliated. All the evils which spring from ill-feeling between the rulers and the ruled will fall upon the country. Therefore it is the imperative duty of all to take steps to stamp out anarchy and unrest, and to co-operate with the Government in the matter. Every effort should be made that the feelings of enmity towards the Government or the British race be rooted out from the minds of the people, specially those of the boys and young men, and their false notions be dispelled; for England and India are both subordinate to the same mighty Emperor, and the English and the Indians are subjects of the same great Empire. The bonds that bind us can never be severed. It is highly necessary that there should be good feeling and sympathy between us. Whatever is beneficial to England is beneficial to us; the interests of England and India cannot be different. If the guardians and teachers of the boys strive heartily towards this end, the result may be highly satisfactory, for the future advancement of the students depends entirely on the teachers. They should be very careful to see that students are not led astray by participating in any political agitation. It does not stand to reason that one should lay the axe unto one's own welfare by following evil advice and at the instigation of others. If we do not take steps even now, dreadful calamity will fall upon the country.

"RANAJIT SINHA (Maharajah).

"NASHIPUR RAJBATI,
' *March* 19, 1910."

CHAPTER X

THE MAHARAJAH'S FAMILY LIFE

As was mentioned in an earlier chapter, the Maharajah married on May 4, 1883, before he had come into possession of his raj, Kamal Kumari, the eldest daughter of Babu Giridhari Lall of Calcutta. The married life of the Maharajah has proved singularly happy, and there is a family of five sons and four daughters.

The eldest son, or Maharaj Kumar, named Bhupendra Narayan Sinha, is a very intelligent young man, and was born in the year 1888. He has received the best modern education, as well as careful training for the discharge of his duties. After passing his Matriculation examination he was admitted to the Presidency College at Calcutta, and in 1910 successfully passed the Intermediate Arts examination in the First Division. He is now working for the B.A. degree. He married on June 3, 1905, Prem Kumari, daughter of Babu Brijmohan Lall of Gaya, and there is one daughter of the marriage, to whom the name of Nirmal Kumari has been given.

The second son, Maharaj Kumar Nripendra Narayan Sinha, was born in 1894, and is described by one who knows him well as "the personification of all that is good and noble." He received his education at the Hare School in Calcutta, and from it he recently passed with much credit the Matriculation examination at the Calcutta University. The credit was all the greater as his studies had

BABU THACKUR PROSAD.

Maharajah's son-in-law.

To face page 136.

been interfered with by illness. He is now being prepared for the Arts examination at the same University.

The third son is named Rajendra Narayan Sinha, and was born in 1896. He is following in his elder brothers' steps, and will proceed to the University at Calcutta in due course. The two youngest sons, named Birendra Narayan Sinha and Jagadindra Narayan Sinha, are at present receiving their education at home.

The eldest daughter is the Maharaj Kumari Basanta Kumari, and she is married to Babu Ram Bahadur, the eldest son of the late Babu Isri Prosad, Reis of Ulao in Monghyr. He has extensive zemindaries in the districts of Mozafferpur and Monghyr, and has also a big banking business in Mozafferpur, which he is managing with great credit since his father's death.

The second daughter is named Hemanta Kumari, and is the wife of Babu Thackur Prosad, zemindar of Chunar.

The third and fourth daughters, named respectively Kassum Kumari and Pratima Kumari, are still minors, but the former has been betrothed to Babu Harinarayan, son of the rich zemindar and banker of Bhagulpur named Babu Govind Sahai.

In the persons of his children the Maharajah of Nashipur is extending the influence of his family among the landed aristocracy of Bengal, Behar, and the United Provinces.

The Maharajah is a devout Hindu with liberal ideas, and in this respect keeps up the traditions handed down by his predecessors. He is universally popular, and is respected by all his officials and dependents. In addition to his business capacity, the Maharajah is distinguished by his cultured tastes and polished manners. Towards his inferiors he is particularly condescending, and he keeps on his office table a small marble slab engraved with the words "Despise none," which may in a sense be regarded as the motto of his life. He is always ready to assist in any good movement, and spends a considerable sum each year on objects for the benefit of the general community outside his estates.

He has a fine library which is enriched with several old Sanskrit manuscripts, and his art gallery contains many good pictures.

Maharani Kamal Kumari is a dignified and accomplished lady, noted for her large-heartedness and disposition to do good to all. She is on friendly terms with most of the distinguished European ladies of the highest rank and position in India, and is loved and respected by all her people, dependents and acquaintances. It is indeed a noteworthy fact that her charitable disposition is always directed to relieve the wants of her dependents, and that whenever there is any illness in any family at Nashipur she always takes great interest in the case and helps the afflicted with money and other necessary assistance. Indeed, she always evinces a deep interest in all matters affecting the moral and social progress of the female sex, and tries her best to ameliorate the degraded condition to which so many Indian women have sunk. Wherever she goes she makes friends with the leading ladies of the place.

Allusion has been made to the religious fervour that has always characterized the heads of the Nashipur family. In this respect Maharajah Ranajit is in no way behind any of his ancestors. He honours the Brahmins, maintains the temples of his ancestors, and largely contributes to the cost of the religious festivals, which are the source of so much gratification and pleasure to the Hindu community.

There are four great festivals each year at Nashipur. They are the Tulsibahar festival, the Ratha Jatra, the Jhulan Jatra, and the Dole Jatra. Taking them in their order, we may attempt to give some details of each of them.

The Tulsibahar festival is one of the important festivals amongst the Hindus, and is celebrated in the month of Jysta, or May. When Rajah Bahadur Sinha established the symbol of the deity Lukshmi Narayan Deb Thackur a Gaisabad at the commencement of the last century, this was the festival that he always celebrated with the greatest éclat, and pilgrims used to attend it from far and wide. It was in connection with this festival that the great fair, or *mela*, which extended over a month, used to be held. This naturally attracted great crowds, and singing and nautch parties were especially provided for the entertainment of the concourse.

Since the removal of the Thackur from Gaisabad to Nashipur, the latter place has become the scene of the festival, the duration of which has, however, been reduced from one month to a fortnight. It still commences on the first day of Jysta, but concludes on the fifteenth day. The amusements provided have been extended, and now include operas, theatricals, and a circus. It is small wonder, then, that the public who pay nothing find the entertainment very amusing, and that the principal supporter of the festival acquires great popularity.

The Ratha Jatra festival is that of the Car, and is celebrated in the month of Ashar, corresponding with our month of June. The Nashipur Rajbati is the central point of the celebration, and the Ratha, or Car, which is made of silver, is about 30 feet high and 14 feet broad. In the morning of the appointed day the Thackur Ramchunder Deb ascends the car, and the same evening the car is drawn by the assembled crowds with great veneration from the Rajbati to Mahimapur. It is the general belief that those who succeed in drawing the car will attain eternal salvation.

While the car is being drawn along the road, a procession takes place alongside it. The procession includes the Raj sepoys armed with guns and bayonets, led horses richly caparisoned, attendants carrying silver huddas, flag bearers, bands of music, trumpeters and drummers. The Maharajah, accompanied by all the members of the Raj family, the officials of his administration, a large number of specially invited guests, and a great body of retainers, walks behind the car for the first part of its journey. After about half an hour's walking the Maharajah and his party quit the procession and return to the residence.

On the eighth day the car is brought back from Mahimapur to the Rajbati under similar conditions and amid a vast concourse. The grandeur of the scene makes a profound impression on the people's minds, and there is no doubt that this festivity not merely sustains the religious fervour of the people, but provides them with no inconsiderable amusement.

The two festivals referred to are quite eclipsed, however, in grandeur by the Jhulan Jatra, which is held in the month of August in each year. This may be compared with the great Durga Pujah festival of the Hindus, and in no other place in Bengal is it celebrated with the same magnificence as at Nashipur. The festival, strictly speaking, lasts for five days during the month of Sravan (August), but the great fair which accompanies it goes on for a much longer period. This festival is one especially of pleasure and rejoicing, from which the religious element is almost entirely absent. For this occasion the Maharajah commissions from Calcutta the choicest and very best Jatra parties and dhaps, just as the great hostesses of English society retain the latest singer or musician for their receptions. It is scarcely necessary to add that visitors in their tens of thousands flock into Nashipur for the event.

It may be explained that a *Jatra* is a singing or dancing party — a combination of theatricals and opera, *i.e.*, a musical performance, consisting of actors, singers and dancers, and accompanied with musical instruments and enriched with magnificent dresses; while a *Dhap* is a purely singing party with musical instruments, generally consisting of a principal female singer with male singers and players.

The festival must rather be compared to a great fair than anything else. The fun of the fair sways the crowd, the god remains in his shrine, and the silver car is not rolled through the streets. On the other hand, the people from Murshidabad, Birbhum, and other districts flock to it, while the Government officials, pleaders, muktars, and all persons with any claim to gentility receive special invitations from the Maharajah. The railway company runs special trains, and the steamer company on the Bhagirathi also places additional steamers at the disposal of the public for the occasion. It very often happens, too, that these companies are unable to provide for the great crowds that wish to be present.

But on this occasion there is a particularly severe strain on the Maharajah's hospitality, for he is supposed to play the host, or at least to provide the bulk of the visitors with accommodation. He appoints his own officers for the purpose, and they are charged especially with the task of seeing that no disturbances take place to mar the harmony of the festivities.

Every night the Rajbati is lit up, and its innumerable lights make a brilliant spectacle, while round the town are the circuses and theatres in which a great variety of amusements are provided for the entertainment of the assembled visitors. While all this is going on outside, a great *majlish* (gathering) of all the invited gentlemen is being held inside the Rajbati by the Maharajah. He attends in person, accompanied by all his family and followers, and makes a great personal effort to see that his guests are properly entertained and provided for in every way. The guests are not merely sumptuously fed, but have their travelling expenses defrayed out of the Maharajah's purse.

The fourth and last of the festivals is the Dole Jatra, or Holi. This is held in the Rajbati, and generally takes place in the month of March on the day of the full moon.

On this occasion, also, good jatras, dhaps, or kirtans, are brought from Calcutta to supply entertainment, and the principal gentry from Murshidabad city, Lalbag, Ichagang, Baluchar, Azimganj, and other places, receive special invitations. On this occasion, also, the Maharajah receives and entertains his guests in person. The Notmandir ceremony held on this night is of special interest, for all the guests and visitors are crimsoned with red abir powder amid cries of "Holi-hai!" signifying "This is the holi day." The next morning the populace assemble in front of the Rajbati, and amuse themselves in a right joyous fashion according to Oriental custom as of yore.

Enough has been said to show that Nashipur is not a dull place, and that the Maharajah is expected to provide popular amusement—sometimes combined with religious ceremonies—as well as to render material help to his people when they need it. It is also perfectly clear that he discharges his duties in the manner expected of him to the complete public satisfaction, for, by all accounts, he is one of the most popular men in Bengal.

We have now passed in review, not only the family history of the House of Nashipur, but also the chief incidents in the public and private life of its present head, the Maharajah Ranajit Sinha Bahadur. The story of this remarkable landowner and administrator is of interest, because it shows that under the torrid sun of Bengal the conditions of life are very much the same as with us. The good landlord is regarded as the general benefactor and the father of his people. In India, the public appreciation takes the form of veneration, and it is consequently impossible to measure the extent of the influence that a man like the Maharajah exercises on those who are in any way dependent on him. But the Maharajah's influence is not confined to Nashipur. He possesses a great hold on the public opinion of Bengal, and that is why his pamphlet on sedition, widely read and freely circulated in the vernacular, produced such a deep impression among the masses which are beyond the reach of Governmental publications.

So far, the Maharajah's work has been chiefly done in his own districts; but his year's experience on the Bengal Legislative Council introduced him to public affairs affecting the largest and most prosperous province of India. He then acquired, not only what is known as popularity with the public, but the respect and goodwill of his English colleagues, both official and unofficial, which may be fairly regarded as the more difficult task of the two. It also qualified him for more important public work whenever an occasion may arise. The support of such men as the Maharajah provides the surest basis for the maintenance of British power and authority in India. The reader will not have failed to note that from the very beginning of the story of Nashipur, commencing with Dovi Sinha one hundred and fifty years ago, loyalty to the British raj has been the most prominent characteristic of all the members of this family.

In concluding this little history, a better ending could not be found than a description of the part that the Maharajah and the whole community of Nashipur took in the Imperial Durbar at Delhi, and the Proclamation of Their Majesties King George V. and Queen Mary as Emperor and Empress of India. That event provides a historical date and landmark in Indian history. There was the great pageant in the old and now the new Capital of India which special correspondents have brought before us; but throughout the whole of the peninsula there were the unchronicled, but not less significant, local celebrations and rejoicings. The following paragraph, contributed by a friend on the spot, tells in a few lines what occurred in Nashipur, and may be regarded as typical of the new loyalty that has been aroused by the Royal visit to India in the hearts of those millions who are our fellow-subjects and brothers in devotion to the glory and upholding of the British Empire:

"Their Imperial Majesties, the Emperor and Empress of India, held the Coronation Durbar at Delhi on the 12th December, 1911. The Maharajah of Nashipur attended the Durbar as a guest of the Bengal Government, and was one of the chosen representatives of Bengal who did homage to their Imperial Majesties.

"The Coronation was celebrated at the Nashipur Rajbati on the said 12th day of December in a right royal style. The Rajbati and all the other houses and the main road at Nashipur were tastefully decorated with flags, festoons and evergreens. Early in the morning a royal salute of one hundred and one guns was fired, and loyal messages of congratulation were drawn up and sent off by telegraph—one from the Maharani, on behalf of the Pardanashin ladies of Nashipur, was forwarded through Her Excellency, Lady Hardinge, of Penshurst, C.I., to Her Imperial Majesty, the Empress of India, and the other was sent in the name of all the people of Nashipur, through His Excellency the Governor-General of India, to Their Most Gracious and Imperial Majesties, on the celebration of Their Majesties' Coronation in their Indian dominions, with deep and respectful assurances of staunch loyalty and devotion to their persons and throne.

"A grand procession started from the Rajbati exhibiting prominently Their Majesties' portraits, decorated with garlands, flags and flowers, and paraded all the principal roads and streets of the town, amidst enthusiastic cheering, chanting hymns especially composed for the occasion, and invoking the blessings of Heaven for their Majesties' long life. Prayers were offered at the Raj Temple for their Majesties' long life and safe and happy sojourn in India, *bhogs* were offered and *prosad* distributed to all.

"Precisely at noon a Durbar meeting was held at the Rajbati under the presidency of Babu Surada Prosad Mukherji,

Dewan, in the absence of the Maharajah at the Coronation Durbar at Delhi, in which all the residents of the town and surrounding places joined. The Royal Proclamation was read, and a speech was delivered impressing upon the people the benefits of British Rule, and exhorting the audience to remain loyal and faithful to the British raj. At the conclusion of the Durbar, the band struck up the National Anthem, and another salute was fired. In the afternoon there were athletic sports by schoolboys, about a thousand poor were sumptuously fed, and the school-children were given a treat. At dusk, the Rajbati and all the houses of the residents, and the principal roads also, were brilliantly illuminated, followed by a display of fire-works at the Rajbati, as well as in many other of the principal houses in the town. At night, there was a theatrical performance by the Bharuti Natya Somaj.

"In all the Mofussil offices and Kutchurrees appertaining to the Raj, the Royal Proclamation was also read, and His Imperial Majesty's portrait exhibited. There were also decorations, illuminations, and a display of fireworks in all these places."

And so, with this loyal scene present in our mind, we close this history of a typically loyal family and raj.

THE END.